*Landscapes
of the
Heart*

Alpine Prospect with Castle, River & Shrine

Landscapes of the Heart

Collected Poems 1970–2019

Djana Bayley

Bywater Press
Bellingham, Washington

Also by Djana Bayley from Bywater Press
The Scales of Astraea: Poems of Earth, Its Creatures & The Old Gods, 2017

© 2019 by Djana Bayley Bock. All rights reserved.
www.djanas-art.com

Published by Bywater Press, Bellingham, Washington.
www.bywaterpress.com

First edition, first printing.   I K L M N
ISBN: 978-1-7330675-0-8

For Two Men

~ ~ ~ ~

*One who returned
and brought back my words
&
One who gave me
space and time to write them*

Contents

Preface xv

Evocations & Elegies

The Faery Isles 5
The Gods Also Give 7
Votary of Dawn * 9
Wings of March 11
Jupiter's Herald * 12
May Zephyr 13
Monterey Fog 14
Summer Wind 15
Swallowtail * 16
Wings Against the Morning * 17
Midsummer Nightmare * 19
Coast Range – Afterimages 20
Mountain Wine 22
Morning Mountain Alchemy 23
September Roses 25
Vintage September 26
'Et in Arcadia' 27
Illyric 28
The Aspen Grove 30
Aeolian Lyre 32
Alpine Light and Wind 33
Winter Light 35
Mountains in Winter 36
Blue Pacific 37
Within Our Gates 39
Gentleman in Bowler Hat 40
The Siffling Wind 41
Chronological 42
The Rope Dancers 43
Starry Infinity 45
Olympic Mountains – A Winter Fantasia 47

* These poems were originally published in *The Scales of Astraea*, 2017.

In Memoriam
    Rachmaninoff – Piano Concerto No. 2 59
    The Orient Express – Exile and Escape 67

Figures in a Dream, Voices on the Wind
    Danaë 77
    Three Winds 78
    Beyond the Well at the World's End 80
    Two Figures in Moonlight 82
    The Faery Lover 83
    The Forest Glade 85
    The Courtly Lover 87
    Black Horse at Sunset 89
    November Storm - Merioneth 90
    Path of the Summer Stars 92
    Alpine Triad – Fragments 94
    Waxwings 95
    Biedermeier Autumn 97
    Souvenir of Old Provence 99
    Concert Hall Rendezvous, 1919 101
    Carniola, August 1943 103
    Warp and Weft 105

The Lost Heart – Wayfaring
    How Many Miles? 113
    Three Young Eagles 114
    Petition 116
    A Thin Wind 117
    The Spiral Stair 118
    Thief of Dreams 119
    October's Forge 120
    November Rain 121
    The Musician 123
    Last Act 124
    To the Kindly Ones 125
    Confetti Snow 127
    Summer Day 128
    The Whetted Blade 129

Heartbreak	130
Chrysalis	131
The Orchard Meadow	132
The Raveled Shift	134
They Loved Me They Said	136
The Small Dun Bird	138
Litter	139
The Iron-Locked Coffer	141
Beyond the Black Curtain	143
The Golden Key	146
Falling Star	148
Two Minute Film Clip	149
Nuclear Winter	151
Soul's Vessel	152
Chain of Fire	154
Gold Suns, Sapphire Oceans	156
Heart's Home	158
Terminal	160
The Way Home	162
At the Fleeting Edge of Dreams	163
Shadows under the Pines	165
Orphan Phantoms, Reaching	166
Sun Blindness	168
Ashes	169
Another Country	170

Foreshadowings

The Tapestries in the Tower	177
A Spirit, Wayfinding	183
The Other Woman	186
Pale Shades and Star Roads	187
The Asphodel Meadow	190

Coda

Cavalier of the Rose	195

Illustrations
(Drawings by Ms Bayley)

Alpine Prospect with Castle, River & Shrine, Carinthia, Early Summer	iv
Cottage at Sunset with Poplar & Fox, Welsh Border Country, Autumn	2
Temple on Headland with Three Dolphins, North Aegean, Spring	74
Castle with Nightingale & Climbing Roses, Old Lotharingia, Midsummer	110
The Cavalier's Silver Rose & Sophie's Handkerchief from *Der Rosenkavalier*	192

Preface

Lost worlds, lost gardens and lost love are the over-arching motifs in *Landscapes of the Heart*. Many of the poems herein contrast the delight of being surrounded by love and beauty in a Paradise Garden with the crushing anguish that can submerge body and spirit when one is shut out of this place of heart's desire – anguish which only increases as one comes to understand that in this life the gods have forever closed its gates against you.

I believe one of the primary psychological conditions underlying human experience is that of Paradise Lost. Only consider – our first experience of being alive in this world comes when we are brutally ejected from the warmth and safety of the womb; thereafter it is as inevitable and certain as life's breath that most of us, whether early in life as a child, or later as an adult, will again find ourselves denied access to some ideal place of perfect felicity. Perhaps this place vanishes with childhood's end, or circumstances remove you far from it, thereby severing you from your heart's dearest love. . . .

Hence quite a few poems in this volume relate the struggles of a protagonist – whether a 'real' person or its soul or ghost – to survive in a world outside one's perfect environment, and the soul's attempts to confound Fate by hazarding a journey or quest into the unknown to seek this garden abode once more – that singular place we always immediately recognize as our heart's true home.

Through the days of my life, many of the byways I have followed have led me a-wandering, lost, through desert wastes, miry swamps, thickets of briars and tangled woods, along barely discernable trails over rocky mountain chains – even to sailing in frail barques over tumultuous seas. Nevertheless at times Lady Fortune, relenting, would set my feet on unexpected paths leading me through sunlit, flower-enameled clearings where crystal streams sparkled; but as an adult, whenever I walk in rainbow meadows filled with bird song and dancing butterflies, I am ever conscious I only need pass a stand of firs, turn a corner and in an eye-blink the vista may change to one of dark clouds piled over dense forests where predatory beasts roam.

The poems in *Landscapes of the Heart* are those I have brought back from a lifetime of exploring these perilous and exquisite lands, countries that lie just beneath the surface of our conscious minds and are profoundly a part of each of us. These places are glimpsed when we dream, whether the dreams emerge in night's sleep hours or drift to the edges of thought in daylight. These are the eternal lands of heart's delight and enchantment, forever vanishing from our sight yet near as the beating heart in each of us.

All manner of folk may be encountered in these lands – dwarves, sorcerers and wise women, princesses in disguise, high nobles and poor peasants, the faerie races, even certain of the old gods who yet walk among us in dreams. As well, people once known who have disappeared from one's life are seen, or who, much loved, are now dead and forever lost . . . at times one might even be shocked by meeting an aspect of your very self, coming toward you or moving away.

Strange, beautiful and deadly animals, birds, and other creatures inhabit these regions as well, and therein one walks beneath unknown trees through scenes oddly familiar and almost remembered, but always along tracks never noticed in one's mundane life. Yet these half-hid byways must be ventured, or our souls starve, for all our life we seek – consciously or unconsciously – the one road that will lead us to our own rightful dwelling place. It is only there a human soul's inborn restlessness will be stilled and peace found at last – and if one is denied this place in 'real' life, glimpsing a vision of it in the Never-Never can, at least briefly, mitigate the despair inevitably rising from knowledge of our mortal condition.

The poems in this book are strongly rooted in three stylistic traditions: old English, Scots and Welsh ballads; English poetry composed from the age of the Tudors through the Romantic era and into the decades-long reign of Victoria; and in the myths and legends from the times of the early Celts and Greeks and on to the eighteenth and nineteenth centuries when the great European and British collectors of fairy and folk tales began recording the old narratives and their later variants.

As a committed artist as well as a poet and a once-upon-a-time dancer, various periods in art and music often provide points of reference; sometimes a specific piece of music or a painting inspires an entire piece. Few end rhymes are found here, nor are traditional verse forms. Instead I employ lines longer than usual in English poetry, and manipulate syntax, rhythm and internal rhyme in my own quirky manner. Such devices, however, always and only serve the main impetus of the poems, which for me is the telling of stories.

Three collections of poems are included in this volume, each expressive of a different primary theme:

Evocations & Elegies: descriptive reminiscences of seasons, places, people and creatures that have become lost to me or vanished entirely from the earth, along with several scenarios concerning the human predicament and the possible future of our race.

Figures in a Dream, Voices on the Wind: the curtain shrouding bygone times parts to reveal fragmented glimpses into lives and events that 'might have been' in eras distant from ours, from the time of the fabled Golden Age, Greek and Celtic myth, and periods in European history from the Medieval through the Renaissance and the Second World War.

The Lost Heart – Wayfarings: the poems in this final section chart the evolving aspects of love – that diamond-complex topic with an infinity of facets reflecting both moods and physical actions. Here is love found, love lost, love bitter and biting, love wry and whimsical, love regained, love eternal – and even after so many poems on the topic I still haven't come to the end of it. How could I? It is the essential foundation of our being, along with the never-ending quest for the lost Paradise Garden.

The stories told in these poems often occur in mere moments, while others take the protagonist – whether ghost or flesh-and-blood human – journeying for days or years in lost kingdoms of the world, or through fantastic dreamscapes – even along pathways leading across the starry heavens . . . all places waiting to be discovered in the enchanted countries lying within *Landscapes of the Heart*.

Djana Bayley
Lynnwood
October, 2019

Ode to a Nightgale, closing stanzas

Thou wast not born for death, immortal Bird!
   No hungry generations tread thee down;
The voice I hear this passing night was heard
   In ancient days by emperor and clown:
Perhaps the self-same song that found a path
     Through the sad heart of Ruth, when, sick for home,
        She stood in tears amid the alien corn;
          The same that oft-times hath
Charm'd magic casements, opening on the foam
   Of perilous seas, in faery lands forlorn.

Forlorn! The very word is like a bell
   To toll me back from thee to my sole self!
Adieu! the fancy cannot cheat so well
   As she is fam'd to do, deceiving elf.
Adieu! adieu! Thy plaintive anthem fades
   Past the near meadows, over the still stream,
      Up the hill-side; and now 'tis buried deep
        In the next valley-glades;
Was it a vision, or a waking dream?
   Fled is that music – Do I wake or sleep?

                              John Keats, 1819

Cottage at Sunset

Evocations & Elegies

The Faery Isles
with Deepest Respects to Alfred, Lord Tennyson

The tall-masted ship crests the swell . . . suddenly,
through thick-glazed, fogged port-holes, rising under
the western wind, mist shrouded glass-green islands

emerge – soft rounded hills sliced by knifing cliffs
fringed below in frothed cream-lace waves crashing over
giant-flung boulders are briefly glimpsed behind

slashing sweeps of rain, fountaining arctic ocean
spume and obscuring vapor smoke of northern
cloud swirled by polar-ice winds . . . moments later,

the ship pitches, slides deep into a yawning,
steep-walled abyss of cascading, marrow-cold,
pewter-green water – the islands disappear . . .

to be continually lost, seldomer
discovered through all Antiquity's pastel
washed blue-green, rose-gold primavera years,

cold, dark epochs Mediæval of iron cruel
ermine, royal purple, ebon satin, and
blood-shot Renaissance gilt brocaded, jewel

glittering decades. Even in distant
star-brilliant aeons before fable, rare the
barques that come intact through these high-mounting,

sickeningly disintegrating seas,
the lancing rain, sword slicing winds, ice-spearing
frost, to sail at last, battered, proud, into . . .

a looking-glass harbor of translucent
aquamarine mirroring lofty bluffs topped
with high-towered castles, their slim, blade-point

spires rising into crystal sharp, wind rinsed
skies where untarnished sunlight dazzles sparks from
metal-capped turrets, gilt weather vanes, wrought

filigree balconies and window surrounds,
and casts a dancing shimmer of rainbow
prisms across mica-infused, silver-white walls.

Silken emerald, sapphire, ruby, topaz
pennons stitched with griffins, lions, eagles,
yales, unicorns unfurl, flutter and snap

in a brisk boreal breeze as triumphant
paean rings from burnished, uplifted throats of
banner-hung brass, bronze, golden trumpets and

echoes to the frost-blue heaven that deflects
the notes back in platinum showers to spill
over turrets, roofs, ramparts of each bright

citadel and the water-imaged ship,
bass and treble staves shattering on the
mirror-silvered bay and arrowing up

  anew in a million fractured motes to
 cloudless empyrean where, falling back, the sound
   reverberates fainter, sweeter again –
    again –
  and finally fainter fading,
 echoes once more fainter, sweeter still.

The Gods Also Give

    Times the gods also give – suddenly gifting
the letters words, unlocking memories' etymologies:

returning . . . a Loire Valley gray morning, spring
rain pending in an affinity of Athene –

above white brick, slate roof chateau in scythed green
meadow, piled platinum cumulus fast vanishes

behind massing sable clouds – in dimming pearl-shell
light, the countless jade, citrine and lime-green leaves

of surrounding groves sheen and gleam while a small,
storm-portending wind hushes through, setting boughs

ruffling and rustling, while following water
droplet patterings stir the argent-stemmed trees'

million leafy tongues to whispering ancient
enchantments through veiling coils of gossamer mist . . .

reminding . . . a summer noon's glare-dazzling southern
light, sun's arrows igniting sparks in glittering

dust motes swirled within hot air currents rippling
over dry gullies, overgrown scrub, stone-hard hills,

cracking the crumbling masonry and mortar in
massive, ruined Roman aqueducts, arches,

temples strewn through Provence, and drenching the cypress
spear-pierced landscape in waves of wild perfume – thyme,

lavender, juniper scents ascending in
shimmering offertory to cold Dian's

silver-white orb, translucent against the layered
sapphire deeps and shifting tidal swells washing

across shoreless, unbounded infinities of great
Jupiter's high arcing ocean-heaven above . . .

unscrolling . . . golden Apollo's opal October
sky, gauzy with sharp-scented, smoke-blue incense haze

floating up from marble altars and wreathing thin ghosts
through bead-screened doors in olden Septimania

where, at the end of cobbled streets and dark,
arched alleys tilting down to stone quays, an

ochre-gold sun sets – the fulgent radiance
pouring from its pulsing, molten core turning

the sea a beaten brass shield mirroring in its
gilded ridges, hammered hollows lateen-rigged boats

and galleys large and small alchemized to shining
metallic toys: masts, prows, ropes, spars, furled sails

coated in scintillant, aureate brilliance by
those rays of blazing, flame-yellow fire diffused

out of the sulfurous incandescence burning
above horizon's distant, spell-charmed Isles of Gold.

Votary of Dawn

The poplar stood on the upslope at street's end, ninety
years votary at veiled Aurora's daybreak altar . . .

now only a void – simple air – where once apricot-
gold diffused from sun lifting above the hill spilled

down tree's teardrop lineaments in a radiant
honey pour of light motes lumining every branch

and least twig to the glowing perfection found in
Books of Hours illuminations new-touched by

monks' sable brushes dipped in coruscating, gelid
gold – the hair-fine tips scattering, with precise,

caressing strokes, flames, darts, haloes, rays, sparks of
sun-gilt brilliance over stiff vellum pages.

Each year, April's unfolding yellow-suffused-lime
green leaves triumphed over morning's gold to create

a lacework, transparent scrim in shimmering,
mirror-back chartreuse . . . weeks later summer-soft winds

stirred currents of ocean coolness through darkening
heart-shape leaves autumn transformed from jade to glowing

amber-topaz shades tossing in equinoctial
gales, the crisped leaf-flakes soon frost-alchemized to

burning, brittle embers setting boughs alight, transfiguring
the tree a torch of rustling gold flame, quenched only when

winter's cold sun burnished creaking, naked branches
the rich tarnished gilt of antique picture frames.

The men with saws and machines that kill took a whole
day to reduce you to raw, ugly stump, then days

more to carve and cart your corpse away. Sky there now
barren, its air a bland blank, but I never look

to street's end without seeing your ghost tremble
in that space, bare slim branches swaying in spring

and winter winds, strong limbs rising, in-curved to
each other from your thick forked trunk and forming

a shape of steepled hands, tapered fingers placed together,
          praying.
         We never listen.

Wings of March

Waiting one cloud-scudding March day
for noisy, diesel reeking bus
at the bottom of a shade cold

city canyon – steel, concrete, black glass
cliffs looming sheer and straight overhead –
I hear a faint, thin crying and look

up to see, small and high, white gulls
circling in a narrow azure slash
of sky, lucent sunlight shining through

feathers, skin, bones, making their floating
wings angel-stainless transparencies –
and with a sudden stab remember

similar sight of distant soaring
gulls in a place lost to me this life,
and the intense rush of happiness

carried on those silver-flickering,
noiseless white wings dazzling with such
celestial radiance against

cumulus cloud-heaped blue atmosphere
deep as infinity, precious and
rare as the cobalt tint used to limn

gentian lakes and sapphire heavens
in jewel-bright mediæval manuscripts.

Jupiter's Herald

Smoke gray kitten – white mustache, cravat, mittens –
scampers down brick walk in storm portending wind
piling blue-black cumulus over jagged range
of cobalt and alabaster peaks . . . atmosphere

currents shifting, the airy towers begin to
disintegrate, western gusts sending clouds fleeing so
swiftly forward the scudding vapors transform
into streaming plumes that mimic some giant corvid

escaped from ancient myth, while ivory-white snow slopes,
gilt-tipped hill and ridge forests, shield-polished silver Sound
change from sunlight to shade beneath the great racing
raven-cloud wings. The kitten – ash soft fur ruffling

to thistle puffs, straight up short tail pluming twice size,
eyes all pupil – suddenly pounces where rustle
shivering along dry grass stalks betrays rushing
passage of an outrider zephyr – elusive

herald of the great Thunder God's darkling approach.

May Zephyr

A vernal May wind – bearing scents of blossom,
bourgeoning green, and nestlings' thin piping,

billowing cauliflower clouds across
cerulean skies and stitching white lace to

ruffled indigo wave tips, festooning swoops
of flame-feathered finches through rain-rinsed atmosphere

and buoying returned swallows airy, elegant
circumlocutions . . . rustles new poplar leaves –

chartreuse, periodot, and palest green-gilt vermeil –
to constant motion, tossing, twisting their wiry

stems to reveal silvered backs while sky-aspiring
branches sway in flickering, shimmering plumes and

sprays that, lifting, raise the ascending thousands of
fluttering leaves into air-twinkling green fountains.

Monterey Fog

Through this misty morning fog horns hooting on
cloud-drowned Puget Sound brings back remembrance of
childhood's lost-in-long-ago Monterey days. . . .

A narrow, high-ceiling bedroom, warped
linoleum floor, faded wallpaper, creaky,
sagging springs on metal railed bed in

a paint peeling, gingerbread cottage
holding a half-century's secrets beneath
crowding pines rooted in encroaching dunes . . .

for hours late and early the child
would lie awake in her warm nest in this
chill room listening to deep bass fog horns

sounding across the gray ocean's crashing surf,
picturing with exact, thrill-delicious terror
huge sea dragons talking each to each and

plunging scaled, long-tailed shapes through vast sea
kingdoms . . . she begins inventing a series
of labyrinthine tales to fit the rumbled

conversations and by vacation's end did
not want to depart — all the hollow-toned
monsters had become her dearest companions.

Summer Wind

Memory stirs with a warm June east wind

bearing
white-crowned sparrows sweet brief singing
in tawny, poppy-sprinkled high grass fields,

tossing
pine needles to silver on coast hills and in yards of
tile roof, stucco frosted, bay-windowed houses,

carrying
a trace of ocean chill infused with the
sun pungent scent drawn from eucalyptus

caplets and gray-green leaves, the trees' fluttering
sickle shades and tall pale trunks barring roads –

long, curved, straight – of California . . .
              my childhood.

Swallowtail

Afternoon splash of wine-gold light across
a mossed rock and plush yellow-brown bee browsing
dark hearts of sunflowers for some reason
brings back myself small, a day I wandered

grandmother's garden: prim white stone edged paths,
old, stout-trunk peach tree, lilies, pansies, daisies,
alyssum – and a giant yellow-striped-black
swallowtail butterfly alighting on my arm.

Astonishment and fear rooted me to the spot –
its body seemed half dragon and its moving
insect feet tickled unbearably – but I
stood statue frozen for long seconds, paralyzed

even this young at beholding close as breath
the tactile, heart-shocking reality of
awesome beauty, yet thrilled to my core it chose
that day to so terrifyingly honor me.

Wings Against the Morning

Just after sunrise one fine summer morning, I sit
on a favorite chair in a corner of my garden space.

First I hear them – a sibilance of treble tseet-peeps
announcing arrival – and soon small shapes can be seen

flitting through hazel branches and fence-top lattice to
the suet feeder . . . startled at my presence so early,

they sheer off, some diving into shrubs, others veering
sideways, scribing figure eights around the Cape Fuchsia –

hunger, though, trumps such skittishness, and first one, then three,
then six settle until eighteen or twenty puff-ball, long-tail

beige bodies are feeding, flittering, pecking each other
on top, sides, inside the wire cage, a dense feathered swarm

of hurry-blurry busyness, always a few turning
about, peering out while voicing those peeping cries. The

sun, lifting higher moment by moment, shines stronger now,
and each feather in this whirligig of fan fluttering-

folding-unfolding wings is back-lit to an alabaster
translucence, calling to mind outspread wings of plump cherubim,

constant attendants on hierarchies of ascendant
angels, floating across the springing curves of domed Venetian

ceilings, and I glimpse all these fanned pinions, great and small,
perpetually back-lit as they open against skyscapes of

billowing gold-edged, lilac-gray clouds parting to reveal
that celestial azure lumining Renaissance heavens.

All at once, never ceasing their piping cries, the bushtits
move off in an airy rolling wave of one after

another up-down flight, disappearing into sun-gilded
foliage and leaving not a single downy breast feather

behind – only a sun-burnt retinal after vision of
stainless, out-span wings transparent against morning light.

Midsummer Nightmare

The causeless fear that can shake
heart and rock bones flowered inside my blood

one warm jasmine-scented
June night at the velvet hem of thickest,

pre-dawn black with the barely
perceptible low, round hooting of a

Great Horned Owl declaring
sovereignty in a nearby alder wood.

Lifting me from dream awake,
the vibration sounded again, closer,

raising hairs on my skin's edge –
instantly conjuring our dark hours

ancient, instinct-sharp terror
of the Presence approaching but unseen.

Coast Range – Afterimages
two Ansel Adams photographs

I.

Always it is the light that
lingers on the inner eye –

flooding range on rounded range
of hills folding ridge in ridge,
slanting down honey-warm sun

shafts pouring liquid citron
prodigally over the scene,
transmuting velvet green pastures,

dust bisque earth in a glowing
solar crucible of soft
burning, lucent amber to

realms of evanescence – all
luminous, gold-dust sprinkled
mystery and enchantment.

II.

Again, inner vision follows
a pale rutted track as it curves

athwart a slope bisected by
leaning post-wire fences, bends
round a bank of tall, dry grasses,

emerges below a poppy
sprinkled, burnt gold field, climbs steep past
scattered, wind torn Druid oaks, then

winds into an infinitely
appealing, paradisaic
distance, beckoning onward in hope

of glimpsing childhood's lost daisy-
white, poppy-orange, meadow-green,
bluebird-sky garden Eden.

Mountain Wine

Throughout the winter the mountains stand remote,
undefiled, defining my horizon while

I, exiled, yearn for the few warm months when I
might thread their cleft secret valleys, ascend

up-tilting sweeps of green, flower-gemmed meadows
to view peaks now aspired to only in mind. . . .

Then, in perfect content, I watch from within
a cirque's craggy arms as dawn's pale primrose light

gradually grows, strengthens over summit rims,
begins spilling down rock cliffs and steep slopes,

transmuting hills, trees, meadows, small lakes to known
shapes . . . as mind brims with sun's golden largesse,

night-stiff bones re-animate, lungs expand
with clean pine resin scent while, advancing

farther, the gold-dust rays pour into forest
hollows and valleys, filling them as mead does

crystal cup on gilded stem, and I become
drunk on honey-potent saffron essence, head

dizzied as amorous god's mortal captive
transported to grand Olympian banquet

and served equal generous, over-spilling
measures of strong, fragrant-spiced amber wine.

Morning Mountain Alchemy

Recollection of earliest morning light growing,
glowing within the Olympic Range can engage
mind's memory a wakeful five a.m. hour when,

after scanning Lieutenant Puget's Sound, I look east
and see overarching gray turning the clear lemon
that presages a perfect child's dream of summer day.

Second by second the sky pales, and far reaching rays
begin to re-animate the uneven rick-rack
mass edging western horizon, first touching tops

of the most prominent four peaks – sentinel-
guardians of my Northwest days. I remember one
particular morning, watching from a vantage high

in their interior, how for merest instants dawn
illumined only the loftiest horned tips of
surrounding mountains, then as sun lifted higher,

the slow infusion of increasing light began working
its morning alchemy, transforming gray rock lilac
and ice white snowfields an opal rose-pink that in turn

metamorphosed to a honey-warm luminescence
spilling over obdurate granite, crumbling scree and
wildflower meadows, flowing in gradual descent

to cover miles on miles of sloping fir forests and
pouring its lucent gilt into gullies and ravines
until citron sifting atoms filled even the most

shaded hemlock, cedar and rhododendron dells.
For several heartbeats the chalice of this palisaded
valley over-brimmed with gold-dust transparence

till a slight, resin-fresh air current stirred, its breaths
disturbing atmosphere's shining surround, and in
an eye blink the radiance emanating from the

sun-mirroring, down-powdering molecules shivered –
dwindled – disappeared . . . and for briefest span I
understood all the seeming solid world – perilous

glaciers, remorseless rock, knifing cliffs, deep pile forests,
silver rivers and spume drifting falls, tenacious
flowers, cold wing-folded butterflies, red-tail hawk

screaming its primal cry in tissue-blue sky – this
entire wide-span vista a veiling scrim, web and weft
wove of the numberless millions of shimmering

mineral and metallic scintillae flashing, sparking
forth from spinning, candescent nebulae whorls blooming,
collapsing, re-forming, and reflecting their numinous

bright to black aeons-warped images within a
universe-spanning crystal scrying sphere suspended
before the Great Enchanter's blazing, star-remote gaze.

September Roses

Waves of scent – deep-piled, velvet layered
perfume of roses rising after

rain transmutes turned earth a richer
umber, slicks gray stone paving beside

ordered borders to sky-reflecting
Virgin mantle blue, while late sun wakes

revelation's flames – amber,
blood red, ruby, vermillion, wine –

in depths of translucent chalices,
the luminant out-welling glow

suffusing every petal in
gilded, satin burnished radiance.

In a monastery garden,
September's roses shake lucid weight

of celestial dew from each smooth
and furled silken petal over

forked, dark soil whiles from their honeyed
inmost centers rises offertory

of sweet spiced incense – precious essence the
wanton breezes waft in transparent veils

up to bell tower, along cloisters, then
insinuate shamelessly through tight

shut chapel, refectory windows
and closed doors in rows of monks' bare cells.

Vintage September

Some quality of clear air's knife-bright
late September light sliced soul one

morning, then gradual incoming of
thin, curled cirrus shreds transforming this

by afternoon to a filmy gold
haze, suggested, for gods-known reason,

an old hand-tinted lithograph
rummaged out of used-bookstore bin. . . .

A chateau in the lost long-ago crouched
somnolent on its hilltop – clustered

white houses round a slender spire
below, poplar fringed road curving up

through down-spinning gold dust motes sifting
onto thick stone walls, crenellations,

towers rising above tile roofs and
sun-warm, vine-terraced slopes where voices

sound briefly in cadenced, full-bodied
calls echoing down decades to prickle

in mind's ear, then dissolve quick as
fuzzed, tingle-edged effervescence of

the best vintage champagne years that bursts
swiftly on tongue and forever disappears.

'Et in Arcadia'

Arcadian memories . . .
whispering down bright autumn
winds blowing from lost mornings
of the world tales of leaf strewn

poplar vales, fallow fields edged
in spired topaz rows, those
tall finials which outline every
pastoral view and frame columned

white temples and a marble tomb:
'Et in Arcadia ego'.

Arcadian memories . . .
drifting down each silver-backed
gold leaf prime through blue vespers
when light falls frangible from

a high celestial dome old
Venetian glass marine glinting
from within its depths that
fluorescent ochre found on

chipped stone urns, lichened walls
and ivied satyrs' faces.

note: the Latin phrase 'et in Arcadia ego' translates as 'I too am in Arcadia' – that is, death resides even in this idyllic place. Nicholas Poussin's painting *The Shepherds of Arcadia* gives visible form to this phrase in its most famous modern interpretation.

Illyric

Anywhere autumn, that cool, reminiscent
Arcadian light may strike . . . perhaps one drowsed

afternoon when, through sky's sharp-angled jewel
blue radiance, the slant of gold-dust sun rays

recall some coastal idyllic of Venetian
Quattrocentro with brittle brass, copper and

later dark Baroque gold leaves drifting down
lucid west winds blowing from old Illyricum. . . .

Easy the fall then into gilt-paint framed landscape drenched
in that favored Claude Lorrain, early Turner

long-rayed, hyacinth light – where out of shimmering
cyan blue Adriatic luminescence

swallow-swift lateen-rigged ships scull oars toward white
Dalmatian port towns perched on steep bleached hills midst

resinous pines and spiked, scent-sharp shrubs – skimming across
azure bays, the barques moor beside marble quays where

in dream slow sequence small aureoled figures
unload rare cargo: Baltic amber, Muscovy furs,

silks and purples of Damascus and Tyre,
Afric diamonds, ivory, gold, Indies spices,

pearls, emeralds, Himalaya tea leaves, Afghan
poppy seed, Kyrgyz carpets, Siam ebonwood and

rubies, and from far Cathay, porcelain and jade –
the bales, barrels, boxes heaping and piling

inside the glass-thin, transparent skin of atmosphere
for a breath-held span . . . until a sudden sea-crisp

September breeze begins shredding the fine membrane,
spinning it to gauze-fine haze above ochre tile

roofs, walls, temples, towers, domes, colonnades built up
and down the precipitous, stony slopes. As

the wind, increasing, tosses spired poplar limbs to
fountaining plumes of clashing platinum, a flame-streaked

sunset blazons transparent cerise and citron
through darkling, violet-layered cloud, diffusing

a saffron-radiant, Illyric incandescence
over topaz offshore islands, lighthouse, harbor

and ships, white-wash buildings, turreted castle on
lofty crag and distant amethyst mountains.

The Aspen Grove

Entire worlds live in the shining leaves
of aspen trees . . . once, in an autumn gold
grove, I walked in sweet, silent harmony

with one since gone from me – the aspens
rustling their secrets leaf to leaf as they did
through lost aeons on untamed hills and moors

of vanished Celtland, when wayward breezes
riffled their quivering leaves constant, hushing
conversation down rocky troll-lurked slopes,

tossed fleeting enchantments, glimmer-sheer,
across emerald boughs twinkling on verges
of trackless woodlands, conjured spells in the

motion of each rounded leaf twisting beside
effervescing ice-green streams rushing, tumbling
down steep-banked glens to faery haunted pools.

Unnumbered millions of pewter-backed, mirror-green
aspen leaves, flickering on flat, pliant stems, have
whispered through countless centuries changing

seasons a sibilant arcana of sun,
clouds, earth, rain, butterflies, beetles and worms,
squirrels, foxes, hedgehogs and badgers to bright-eyed

birds, their flighty chatter scattering the tales
on frisking winds to uplands suffused with
honey-lucent shafts of light slanting through groves

shivering in shifting currents of sharp-edged
late summer air – revealing the restless
viridian, argent-backed leaves beginning

their annual transformation to treasure coin
glitter-bright as new mined dwarf-delved gold soon
to be flung, blown, swirled in rippling whirlpools of

atmosphere, then – drifting, dropping back in
dazzling thousands – strewing crystal-dewed, star and
moon illumined clearings where mushrooms sprout in

spectral rings and the pale gray, straight-stemmed trees
last leaves dapple shifting diamond shadows while
air-sifting silver-gilt gleams spangle fur, glint in

eyes of long-eared, mad hares and night's elfin-wild
creatures frolicking lunatic beneath
a round equinox moon, her gaze cold and white.

Aeolian Lyre

Each year the winds of October arrive from
darker, remoter spaces, their chill breaths carrying

scintillant motes of aeons' disintegrated
landscapes through hollow distances of blade black light.

Occasionally an impulsive wind god gathers
certain of these atoms into haphazard air currents

that gust fleeting mirage-wraiths of lost worlds, forgotten
kingdoms, fragmented cities through earth's streets, forests,

and meadows, along narrow paths, byways and lanes . . .
but instantly as visioned, these phantasms vanish,

though their trailing, diaphanous veils diffuse a spiced
grape-wine perfume that lingers smoke-traced moments

after, while other days ripples of cool pellucid
ozone stir the fading field, meadow, woodland

tapestry to a faint trembling, the thinning
weave of yellow and orange, rust, brown and purple

flickering here and there with the jewel-bright translucence
of sun-infused stained glass, while a sudden shiver

on the edge of consciousness lifts skin hairs when – at
the farthest verge of hearing – surrounding atmosphere

tingles with a high chiming shimmer of wind-tangled
celestial scales – treble clef violet notes singular to

white-haired Aeolus's platinum and diamond lyre,
and plucked, riffled, spilled from its silver-cold wires by

the god's long-fingered attendant zephyrs to enchant
the defenseless hearts of this planet's mortal children.

Alpine Light and Wind
A Bacchanal

Occasionally the bright wind blowing in
October recalls some lost alpine duchy,
long forgotten borders vanished with
the old Austro-Hungarian Empire.

Borne on golden wings of Boreal wind,
early light spills over a circling rim

of granite peaks – irridates blue-white ice
diamonds deep in frozen glaciers – kindles

flickering opals in shadows on
snow – pours liquid amber over spear

sharp firs marching in stiff battalions up
and down steep slopes – ignites glowing topaz,

garnet, ruby-red foliage torches on the
valley plain and polishes the dark pewter

river winding there to glinting silver – pricks
gold flames on tips of needle-thin spires rising

from huddled brown villages – wakes a thousand
tiny dandelion seed-head fire embers

to dazzle and dance over an abbey's plump
copper domes, strikes citron sparks off its

filigree gates – and scatters points of spangled
radiance through the surrounding town off

gilded clock hands, weathervanes, scrolled wrought iron
signs, copper shingles – flares into sheets of

ochre-rose flame on bow-fronted shop windows –
brushes a luminescent palette of hues

over fresco-painted walls – and flushes
dew-gemmed, rainbow tints across petals of

ghost flowers nodding in window boxes and
stone urns set around a fountained square . . .

all whiles white-haired Boreas's wind
swirls its transparent veilings of air –

compound of sun, high altitude ozone,
crystal chill water, sharp-cut granite, quartz,

mica rock dust, spiced pine resin, crisped motes
of lime, beech, birch, oak, chestnut leaves – through

villages, abbey and town, along back lanes
and down twisting, cobbled streets where its fragrant

breath, wafting upward, filters through casements
of octagon-paned windows – stirs fringed curtains

cross-stitched in vivid beast, bird, flower, heart
motifs – and fills a hundred and one small,

dark-raftered rooms with a pungent incense
intoxicating as new-vintage wine.

Winter Light

Knife blade thin, winter sunlight shafting from
sky of palest ice blue satin rinsed platinum

at zenith diffuses in its arc across
salt water Sound an even silver-white

luster streaked here and there with chill
aquamarine, though the no-color

silvered brightness prevails at island edges,
perfectly mirroring beaches, steep cliffs

and teal-green forests crowning island hills,
while the overall filtered silver-white

light lumines peninsula foothills beyond
and above these, on western horizon,

the Olympic Mountains, casting each peak
into stark relief so that every facet

in each mass – lancet pointed summits, sharp-slant
inclines, spiked rock ramparts, granite spined ridges,

escarpments and ledges, cut-diamond snow slopes,
shadowed gullies and crevasses – is at once

separately disclosed and projected with
the startling contrast and keen precision of

an old master etching incised against the
cool gray of a northwest coast December day.

Mountains in Winter

Seen or unseen their presence stalks my days.
Always aware of them defining western

horizon, impulse to chart fluctuations
of light describing those distant slopes through

a day's hours constantly teases my mind,
sending me delving deep, word prospecting.

This winter morning, just before sunrise, the
mountains float dry-brushed insubstantial shades

in tones of gray above a Sound entirely hid
beneath gray-white fog layers until, with sun's

lifting, their faceted east faces flush pink
opal amethyst – evanescent tint that

metamorphoses in seconds with light's
increase, each peak in the jagged range changing

to a detail-precise etching: zinc-white snow,
granite rock shadow-sliced by steep crags, knife-edge

cliffs, pointed pinnacles, plunging ravines – all
this geometry of ice crystal, stone and

scree poised to shatter and impale invaders
unwise enough to venture ascent this

chill, stringent season . . . though I believe stark
fright alone might easily kill at nearer

sight their perilous ice-white, steel-blade blue,
implacable and glittering perfection.

Blue Pacific

In sleep once, twice a year, I am beside my father –
waving, sun-streaked brown hair, Lindberg grin, silver wristwatch,
brown leather flight jacket – inside the vibrating

cockpit bubble of a silver propeller plane.
At ease, privileged as a minor god, I survey
five hundred spacious miles of sea and sky to globe's

remote horizon where blue ocean curves beneath
infinite sapphire space – panorama viewed through
thick Perspex set in thin-skinned metal nose forward

stiff, extended wings glinting sun-struck platinum gilt,
twin propellers each side a whirling blur. We fly through
atmosphere so perfectly clear there seems nothing there,

yet it sustains the plane in a limpid buoyancy
of blue – pale cyan just beyond the glass, but shading
with every mile of distance through the chromatic scale

to darker blue tones. Dotted about the sky, some near, some
at world's edge, enormous whip-cream cumulus mountains
marbled gray-white and lavender-blue float, flow, pile

into spired cloud castles, towers, domed cities
that shifting air currents continually topple then
instantly build up anew into more fantastic

shapes, while far below ocean's wrinkled skin displays
a constantly altering geography of swells
and troughs on a vast patch-work stitched in glittering

blue-spectrum hues: blue-green, blue-royal, blue-violet,
blue-slate, and that darkest indigo blue-black only
seen above ocean's plunging, fathom's deepest trenches.

Always we fly above the tropic Pacific –
the chains of atolls, coral reefs and small, sun-dreamed
islands that were my father's personal Bali Hai . . .

from seabird vantage I watch blue ocean change tint where
it rings our destined island; as we descend, water
shades in demarcated rings from deep cobalt to pure

azure to translucent aquamarine, and I
discern white-tipped breakers rolling onto a sand shore
sparkling diamond white in sun, tall palms in green jungle

fringe engraved crisp as those on three-cent stamps, top-knot
fronds swaying in slight breeze, with narrow runway strip just
beyond . . . the plane banks, turns to approach – and here,

every time, my mind jerks – I spiral back to earth, crash
into consciousness, claimed, chained by gravity again,
my father gone from me once more into the wild blue yonder.

Within Our Gates

Somehow I never think of my Mother
as growing old, but touching her cheek

tonight at departing it felt the soft
paper-fine texture remembered

from grandmothers' kisses, and on the
drive back I fought drowning sadness,

knowing at night in bed alone
with the old cat she must be often

awake, near paralyzed, aware she
shares house space with One standing forth

more visible with each heartbeat that
labors through the winged seconds of

a day's span – that Presence we strive all
our lives to ignore, who waits, patient,
its always approaching hour.

Gentleman in Bowler Hat

Unlike harried Dame Illness,
always bustling to another ward
while you are repeatedly ringing
for juice, chicken soup, tissues,
bedpan, a paperback, the next pill –

Death, that affable gentleman,
is a constant visitor in the room with you –
hanging around, bowler in hand, waiting
for your mutual departure.

Anytime will do, for him.

The Siffling Wind

We'd all begun to conspire belief
in her immortality. Ninety-two years –
a life well-lived, cherished, valued by many.

No cause to mourn beyond reason, I know,
though that small chill wind always siffling at
planet rims and through blank black interstellar

spaces comes tickling edges of my neck
oftener now with every passing hour.

Chronological

Time dissolves around us as we move through
our life – unconscious swimmers thrown in
a deliquescent ether. Our least breathing

motion constantly pushes away our
surrounding, eternally deconstructing
envelope of chronology, perpetually breaking

life's seconds, hours, years into an outward
curving wake of receding occurrence
that winds of circumstance occasionally

blow back over our thin skin in salt stinging
flecks of sharp remembrance – specks that quickly
evaporate as we swim on, heedless, into our

skin, blood and bone designed disintegration.

An uncomfortable chronological
condition natural to our transient race,
and unconsidering of approaching

alteration as soap globes foamed in water
filled bowl and blown careless through child's bubble
wire to bob, drift, spiral, twirl, mingle in

iridescent dance, indifferent of frail
membrane sheaths that will soon burst, dissolve,
vanish, each last one into airy nothing.

The Rope Dancers

The gravid force holding this blue-green globe to its
rightful orbit, the solar energy rotating

its nights to days, tilting seasons hot to cold – that
magnetic, nuclear power will spin planet

onward millennia more, even if the small sphere
circling its insignificant sun is transformed a

frozen orb of crystalized ice . . . likely consequence
our race's unweaving, strand by tensile strand, the taut

plait of cause-effect, birth-death, growth-decay sustaining
the planet's dense-textured, rainbow-inwove braid of life.

We are become rope dancers dangling from high strained cords,
gyrating graceless above stump-burnt, slaughtered forests,

polluted oceans, poisoned rivers, trash and plastic
strewn beaches-marshes-prairies-woodlands-meadows-mountains –

joyless aerialists swinging without nets edge to edge
above opening crevasses, subconsciously aware

the slender cables holding our weight fraying faster
every passing year-month-day-hour unto that

terminal minute when seconds' catastrophe
will sever our lifelines – all the while refusing, in

hubris and blinkered ignorance, to undertake
meaningful labor of repair and restoration.

As we pendulum back-forth, on each swing the widening
chasms of ebon black gape more visible below . . .

panic grips as we stare into fathomless deeps
illumined with flashes of brimstone orange, vulcan red,

atomic yellow, cornea-blinding white, sun
nimbus platinum. . . when our rope fibers jerk in

final whipping unwind, great howling, screaming clamors
rise unto ultimate moment when sharp snappings of

last threads plummet us straight to hell-fired holocaust,
and only the sound of flames, consuming, remains.

Pluming smoke, steaming fogs conceal sky and sun . . . any
life left – bug, lichen, least microbe – dies . . . in silent dark,

beneath sabled pall of cinders and ash, the globe chills . . .
soon, moisture coalesces into ice drops, and gray

clouds begin weeping black tears that streak down in billions
to splinter on hot, vulcanized ground with a constant

hissing susurration . . . through acid-fumed, umbrageous
centuries, swirling around the globe in wind driven

billows and curtaining swathes, frozen sleet falls . . . slowly,
earth's fires quench, and grain by grain the ice particles

cohere, forming thick, gelid sheets that cover mountains,
plains, hills, valleys, rivers, seas, skeletal cities and

towns until the black shroud wicks all water from air, hard
freezing every molecule of wetness. Cloud free, the sphere

encased in glittering carbon winding sheet spins on
its appointed track to last wobbling gyres when sun

itself dims, and the entire minor solar system, collapsing, is
compressed within a black, lead-weighted coffin of whirlpooling
    neutrons.

Starry Infinity
to van Gogh's sun-blazed genius

Light beams in amber-orange-gold spectrum shimmer at the
burning heart of sunsets lingering over the Paradise
Garden where dwell twilight's nymphs, the Hesperides. There

grows Hera's joy, her dragon-guarded tree bearing apples
of gold . . . stray aureate ray deflected from one perfect globe
transmutes into lightning bolt and streaks through shade-obscured

centuries, emerging to infuse the glowing golden
infinities Byzantine icon painters layered
behind stylized landscapes, touched around angels and

hieratic saints' heads and onto holy vessels. This
sunset tint mixed into the gelid gilt Medieval
masters brushed on illumined manuscripts and countless

wood altar panels where it dazzled about edges
of angels, saints and Holy Families, while later
Renaissance and Baroque artists lavishly employed the

lucent hues to outline cherubim and sacred figures,
glisten in rays streaming from Godhead, Son and Holy Dove
on canvases and frescoed chapel walls, and glint in

countless ceiling dome skyscapes where sun and cumulus rims
glimmer and nimbuses gleam around celestial
beings, gods and royals in their ranked, ascending tiers.

Continuing in direct flash, the sulphur-golden slant
fell on Altdorfer, Lorrain, Cuyp, Friedrich, Turner in lucid
succession before striking this genius-afflicted

late nineteenth century artist. No wonder the man
suffered mad intervals, staring as he often dared
with eyes wide open into sun glare and meteors

until day-to-night sky-shell cracked mind wide, near-blinding
him from retina-expanding light that seared his shocked
consciousness to star-fire radiance he slathered

over canvas in impasto-layered citron, saffron, ochre,
red pigments less smooth than older, fine-textured gold, but
close kin in candescent effect. In a shatter of

bursting prisms, throbbing Provençal sun scatters broken
blond darts on peasant and horse ploughing clotted March earth
behind mauve poplar screen, pulses summer fever-heat

in hard cyan sky back of spired, writhing cypresses,
contorted olive trees, junipers, heat-cracked gray rocks,
blood-drop poppies, while in the hot, star-streaming nights,

distant suns spin, planets flash, shooting stars flare above
an indigo river, their myriad luminous sparks
falling into cobalt-black water where the million

> splintering refractions shiver and burn,
> > unquenched.

The light in his vision expanded faster than brush
and palette knife could exorcise unto those last
hours when sun blazed with such scorching, unshielded

power it transformed carbon-blue sky and topaz-gold
cornfield into negative reverse shades of dense, savage
brilliance that, as Destiny's arrow flight of crows advanced,

> the dark-fired effulgence exploded in his brain,
> > consuming him entire.

Olympic Mountains – A Winter Fantasia
Verse Fable in Seven Parts

I.

Slicing ice-edge keen from glacier-carved peaks of horizon
remote mountains, morning wind air-etches crisp image of
world's vanished Pleistocene – knife-blade granite palisades, snow

cornices, blue ice caves, sheer crags and crevasses, rock outcrops,
forested slopes unmarred by man – but within an hour this
unsullied scene transforms, clouds rolling in from west suggesting

a more fantastic vision: mist-wreathed, elf-haunted forests, troll
infested slopes, dwarf-delved alps where swirling vapors conceal-
reveal gauze thin chimeras of Aasgard's fabled, sky-lofty

realm where the Old Gods of the north dwell in enormous gold- roofed
halls and high-raftered lodges: Odin All-Father, raven
on each shoulder, his wife Frigg, and their contentious progeny.

II.

The clouds increase, darken, rain obscuring mountains and foothills
behind gray scrim, though to the northwest winter sun rays begin
slanting through the still falling shower – a rainbow forms, arcing

over Olympics into the swirled, higher-piled cumulus
massed above. I imagine walking from my door downhill to
fir grove where rainbow base hid, there stepping on bright-burning

Bifrost's ribbon prism bridge, climbing higher and higher
over trees, salt water, hills, rugged rock peaks, on and on
higher yet to finally arrive before Valgrind, ancient gate

of the Gods' home where Heimdall the Watcher, high-seated on his
huge, gold-maned horse, burnished gold horn hanging from saddle, grins
   down
at such a presumptuous atomy, gold teeth flashing. I stand

frozen until one cold gray eye winks, then passing between two of
the mirror-polished steel gate columns behold, amazed, Valhalla's
countless towers and turrets, ramparts and walls appearing and

disappearing among floating clouds, the gold-roofed Warriors' Hall
rising highest, Odin's great eagle circling above. In the
forecourt, the immense tree Glasir is rooted, scintillant sparks

from nine million fire-gold leaves making eyes water – blinking,
I glance past tree, espy enormous gray wolf standing guard by
gigantic doors, but he does not stir from post, though muscles

clench beneath the coarse gray fur, and when I move away, legs
wobbling, its head turns, the eyes following my steps gleaming
green-red balefire. The tension-poised wolf, the racket made by

the heroes carousing beneath Valhalla's great roof hurries
me along track skirting fortress's far-flung perimeter
whiles telling myself though I'd not stand chance against wolf, even

if one of those mead-drunk, battle-mad hunks staggered out to piss
from one of the five hundred doors set all round, their crossed eyes would
not spy entity small as I. Only half convinced, I pass

more gigantic lodges, towers and keeps unmolested, but
find myself oft-times glancing back to make certain the wolf not
padding after. As I begin to despair of ever reaching

beautiful Freya's Celestial Fields, a great stag with
majestic antler rack bounds past me to distant wall of dark
slate. With smooth leap, the hart clears barrier, instantly gone from

sight, and I hasten after, certain this wall protects meadow
I seek. Approaching, I locate no entry or gate, but dare
not attempt scaling it – the great boulders prove gray-black clouds

mortared with incessant, repeating lightning streaks that flash
lethal electric-white volts. Farther along wall, I come on
portal formed of arrow-straight bolts jolting down and coursing up

again beneath lintel of roiling thunderheads – but each
flaring rod sizzles so near the next there's no room to slip
between. Well past this fizzing gate, I subside on blue-green grass,

head bowed, useless tears trickling, when a persistent crunching
impinges and eyes lift to a large hare, pearl fur silver-tipped,
grazing quite close. I watch it munch till it sits abruptly,

ears a-twitch, then darts along wall to spot where gray-black cloud
boulders spill forward onto grass. Powered by strong hind legs, the
creature springs up rock-cloud slope, disappears. Moving to this

broken section, I descry no least spark of levin mortar
here and follow, scrambling up the squishy rocks. Poised atop,
I watch the hare join drove of his kind dispersed amongst grass tussocks

in a sky country spreading for leagues on leagues before my
wondering vision – a place of radiant, untarnished
sunlight where low, swift-moving clouds constantly alter the

prospect as they flow over terrain rising-subsiding
into mist-dissolved distance. Squinting, I make out faint line of
mountains beyond a vast plain starred with winking pewter gleams –

likely a river's meander. Nearer, lush blue-green meadows are
brushed purple, blue, rose, primrose and white, and my sight pleased by
cerulean, copen, teal-green, viridian clouds contoured into hedges,

copses, lofty specimen trees while glinting silver streamlets
thread capricious courses and platinum arrows strike my eyes from
glittering surfaces of ponds and lakes scattered through the spacious

meadows, gentle hollows, and sheltered dells. Squelching down vapor
boulders, I lose footing on nothing, tumble to bottom then
   stand back up, unhurt, and commence my wayfaring in
        Freya's exquisite Cloud Country fields.

III.

In flowery leas and shallow vales, I drift amongst lupine spires
touched every blue hue imagined, scented spirea and wild
lilac, their nodding panicles dense with tiny scented florets,

tall star asters displaying fringed ruffs of amethyst and
azure, downy umbellifers ringed in delicate doilies
of white lace, and everywhere daisies short to tall, moon-white and

sun-gold. I discover south-facing dales filled with cream, pale
yellow, blush pink satin-petal poppies; rove along banks of
brooks and pools a-glow with spills of glossy buttercups and

bell flowers in sky shades light to dark nodding on thread stems
amidst plumes of pink astilbe; locate beneath cumulus
hedges and tree canopies cyan, mauve, purple and white

violets, wind flowers and forget-me-nots. Enchanted, I
collect posies of this floral abundance, culling chartreuse ivy
tendrils from cloud tree trunks to bind the stalks, or plucking cirrus

fern from shady banks to surround the blooms, but soon as arranged,
colors in the pretty bouquets fade, then petals, leaves, stems
disintegrate to faintly perfumed dust. Dismayed, I pick no

more flowers from the Goddess's fields, but instead wander at
whim, stroking silken petals, breathing subtle scents, watching gold
and silver fuzzed bees zoom their air tracks among pollen-laden

blooms while myriad butterflies, microscopic crystals in
sun-brushed wing scales revealing ever-changing patterns of
iridescence, flirt and flutter around favorite flowers.

Bevies of quail proceed across fields, mothers leading young to
concealment in gold-tasseled grasses, rose-flushed finches flit, hop,
eat, sing in bramble hedges laden with purple-blue berries

and ground creeping cloudberry vines dotted in segmented gold-
amber fruit, and I laugh quietly witnessing dust-bathing
plump, white-speckled-gold ptarmigan toss mica sparked sand over

ruffled-out pinions, while dozens of while male snow buntings –
wings black-streaked, eyes, bills, legs coal-black – warble sweet and brief
   from cloud
trees before whole flock swoops to feed in fields. Dainty golden deer,

large dark eyes catching light, peer from dappled groves, rust-red foxes,
cravats, stockings, tail tips cream, tumble and yip near dens on the
steeper rock slopes, or streak – brief glimpsed orange flames – across green
   glades,

and cinnamon squirrels, fur red-gold in sun, plumed tails longer than
bodies, scamper up-down hazels, plucking, stripping, cracking,
eating the nuts they search out amongst serrate green-gilt leaves.

IV.

Tiring of walking, I lie on close-nibbled turf beside a
clear pool, studying constantly altering cirrus, cumulus,
stratus clouds, or sit watching their swift metamorphoses in

the pellucid water as little aquamarine, silver
and gold fish flick over cloud forms under the mirror-glass
surface. Stately blue and gray herons, sheen-silver feathers

sweeping from back head down long necks, stand statue still in lowest
lying ponds, contemplating clouds and fish, or stalk on silver-
scaled legs among stiff reeds and triangular stem sedges

before abruptly extending long necks to spear blue-green frog
or fish. Turquoise-blending-teal swallows, throat and breast striking white,
forked tails boasting long streamers, swoop above, beaks snapping on

emerald and sapphire bees, slim demoiselles and heavy-
bodied dragonflies that often sudden-stop darting flights to
suspend near-motionless on gleam-translucent wings

veined crimson, silver or gold. Now and then, at the largest lake
great white swans with black bills and obsidian eyes arrow down
to paddle, preen, bend long necks and admire their reflections

before flying off again, and in lingering twilights and
indigo nights, three of the owl kind hoot and glide in silent
flight: one a small gray, black feathers spotting smoke breast, sleepy eyes

half-lidded in day, at night wide, perpetually surprised – a
larger with upright ear-tufts and streaky plumage providing
perfect camouflage betrayed only by startling gold ringed eyes –

and a majestic white with black beak, eyes, feet, its feathers of
such snowy purity starlight curves to a glowing halo
ringing the ghost shape sweeping through darkness on silent white wings.

V.

One morning early I set out to reach a place where sight might
be attained of glinting water and mountains I spied from wall
the day I entered Cloud Country. Traversing meadows, glens, woods,

I arrive finally at chain of low hills and climb the highest – and
from this vantage behold towering peaks piercing tremendous cloud
banks on farthest horizon, while in the immense plain stretching

from those jagged summits, a broad river – the tint of gelid
old gold in afternoon light – swings in broad s-bends to curl
past hill where I stand. Hypnotized, I watch grasses of the great

prairie bend and rise with the flow of clouds and wind – just across
river, a peregrine hangs pendent, tail fanned, wing-tips fingering
head wind, then he screams, dives into the grass sea. As the sun

slides west and shadows lengthen, I trudge back to familiar
meadows to sleep, but the prospect east fascinates and every
few days draws me back. I observe massive gray-black clouds piling

over the alpine range, and lightning followed by hollow
echo-booms of thunder. Some days my eyes perceive distance-shrunk
beast shapes moving on those remote slopes – white bears treading slow and

ponderous, fast-flowing packs of shadow-gray wolves pursuing
herds of fleeing deer. Hawks and eagles with huge wing-spans spiral
high over peaks and plain, and white gyrfalcons marked with black

dashes on back, wingtips, tail streak fast trajectories, then dive.
Once I glimpse white lynx, fur gray spotted, chasing gold doe and
ivory leaf-blotch fawn through grasses bending in silver

wind-waves while no least breeze touches me. But no matter levin
strikes and thunder crashes in far mountains, or how winds blow
over the plain, in Freya's domain no tempests roar, though

occasionally pearl-gray clouds form and a crystalline rain
falls that neither chills or drenches, and I rejoice in the
fresh scents rising from earth, grass, flowers. Nor ever here do I

notice owls or russet-cream foxes catch and dismember
squirrel or hare, instead subsisting on quail and the ruby-eyed
silver mice scurrying and squeaking amongst leaves, stems and roots.

VI.

So much beauty to astonish, marvels to observe, the days
fleet past, my senses expanding their powers of sight, hearing,
smell, touch, taste. When I hunger, the cloud and bramble berries I

gather satisfy, and when I thirst I cup hands and drink from
clean streams. At twilight, as evening primroses unfurl, rays of
peach, violet, gold and cerise float in misty veils across

the meadows. Twirling within these translucent streamers, I wrap
myself in gauzy radiance then seek place to sleep on plush sward
near perfumed shrub, lying and gazing at star lamps blazing cold

fire more vividly each darkening second while in the chill
brilliance damp grass takes on the sheen of polished graphite and the
cavorting hares' fur turns palest argent. Rare midnights I wake,

and listening to white owls' velvet hoots and the small grays' low
whistles, gaze on a dazzling vision of moon anemones
in their thousands unfolding on shadowed banks and woodland

margins, the luminous candescence welling from their white
chalices competing with the cut-diamond brilliance of the
stars moving on their ancient pathways above. Always, ghost-wan

first light wakes me, skin tingling as the rainbow swathing dissolves –
often several warm-furred leverets are pressed close to me,
their small hearts pulsing against my skin. As stars fade, some mornings

I wade through dew-spangled fields slowly reverting blue-green,
hurrying through vale and wood to hills by the great river. The
yellow glow increasing, I observe light alchemize water

from molten silver to molten gold . . . hardly breathing, I wait.

VII.

As sun's disc lifts above horizon, far across the plain the
tiny figure of a stag appears. Running fast as the slant-
bladed light rays reaching toward Freya's domain, its body, head,

antlers gilt-outlined, the stag grows larger and larger, until
Eikthyrnir suddenly vaults the river in one glorious
long-stretched jump and rushes past me. Hasting after, I see him

drink at glimmering pool exact moment water modulates
from dawn opal to daylight crystal. Replete, the stag turns.
Sometimes, if I keep quite still, he steps delicately near,

looks direct at me and briefly dips his noble head before
bounding away once more. Released from breath-baited spell, I rinse
face, drink from brook, and the day swiftly passes observing,

listening. The hares are quite tame now, eating and boxing
close by me, and buntings and finches, unafraid, sing from near
branches of shrubs while deer, foxes, squirrels go about their lives

regardless of my presence. My soul brimmed to overspill with
wonders, a strange lassitude begins creeping through my veins and
each morning I find it more difficult to rise. Soon – tomorrow

perhaps – I will pluck leaves of cloud fleece from low branches of the
cloud trees and shape a pillow bed by one of the crystal teardrop
pools with movements so languid twilight surprises . . . after

gathering sunset's tinted veils into rainbow shroud I will
sink into the empyreal cloud-down cushions . . . comforted
by drowsy murmurings of quail and ptarmigan, and the

owls' low vocalizations, I watch hares play, fox kits wrestle . . .
as the first stars begin to burn my heavy eyelids close,
my heartbeat slows and I will sleep my last hours away,

      pricking consciousness drowning at last
    in the rising, satin-lucid waters of oblivion.

In Memoriam

Rachmaninoff – Piano Concerto No. 2
composed 1900-1901

Overture

Almost too popular from the first and for a time dismissed by
avant-garde critics – brain-washed devotees of the god Progress – as
hopelessly retrograde, this concerto stands as exclamation
point marking an epoch's ending. From Mozart's time through

revolutions and convulsions Napoleonic, Prussian,
Austrian, Italian, Balkan to the Great War's beginning,
heart-break melodies fountained forth one after another from
seemingly inexhaustible over-flowing springs of

inspiration throughout central and eastern Europe, spreading
a web of tributaries that poured simple to complex-cadenced
rhythms and harmonies into a wide river of sound so deep
the Western world took as granted its lyric flow would never cease.

But *fin de siècle* avant-garde, finding merit only in
deconstruction of every canon in Western art, professed boredom,
scorning as passé this artifact of withered romanticism.
Here, at twenty-first century's beginning, the concerto strikes my

ears as moving memoir of a world and way of life extinct as the
dodo bird . . . certainly it only could have been written by an
artist inhabiting Eastern Europe in that uncertain time and
inspired by the *zeitgeist* to coax those soul-stirring melodic themes

from Apollo's silver-stringed lyre, gifting us a passionate score
foretelling that world's collapse and voicing its most poignant lament.

> As I listen, the music brings forth a vision belonging to
> a world's ending. . . .

Lands of the Eagles

A deep toned bell tolls once, again, and once more again from the gold,
onion-dome cupola of the church on promontory above
a broad south-rolling river; plains stretch away hundreds of versts
either side to remote east and west horizons where clouds mass in

livid cobalt and gray shades, piling on each other to immense air
castles and towers constantly tumbling and rebuilding over wide
rivers and the immense sea of grain and wild grasses interspersed with
white-walled monasteries and small hamlets – izbas, sheds, a wood church,
   geese

and chickens wandering muddy street. In spring, in stream-fringing birch
   groves,
butterflies dance above carpeting bluebells, while in vast pine, ash, elm
forests ferns uncoil, morels sprout, deer give birth, shaggy bears roam and
wolves, muzzles raised, howl at the rising of a full-orbed equinox moon.

Leagues on leagues west, a church with thin, needle-sharp spire perches atop
green rise in an alpine valley, white-washed walls brilliant against gray
rock peaks, knifing cliffs and steep slopes covered with dark green firs and
   blue-green
spruces where goats, shepherd watched, graze; a silver-white cascade falls
   over

granite precipice into river frothing through lush pastures scattered
with tidy brown chalets and browsed by belled cows, every green meadow
speckled with shimmering yellow-red-blue-purple pointillist petal
dots, flittering butterflies, iridescent-winged dragonflies, and

vibrating with humming bees until huge, storm-portending thunderheads
gather above snow-capped summits, some snagging on high peaks while
others begin rolling foaming waves of chill vapor down mountainsides
to drown hills, ridges, valleys in a sea of obscuring fog.

In each zone, west and east, numbers of the royal eagle clan soar
   on rising thermals, surveying their wide-spread territories:

Golden Eagles patrol west, high over Central and East Europe
from the Vistula and Niemen where these flow into the steely
Baltic, north to Tallinn and the Narva gliding into the Gulf of
Finland, then farther still where Onega glints to the White Sea, flying

as well over countryside, marshes, forests from Danzig to Vilna, the
West Dvina, and round Warsaw and Minsk down to Prague, then across
Danube to Linz and above the jagged alpine spine to Graz,
some following the great river's snaking line through descending hills

to Vienna at the rim of the Hungarian plain, then on
south-east to Budapest . . . other Golden Eagles fly over
Central Europe's southern lands, soaring with upswept wings over the
Julian Alps and down the limestone chain to Split on the turquoise

Adriatic, some winging east to Sarajevo and on to country around
Belgrade and into the flat plain of Banat that rises into steep, crevice-
cut fir-covered slopes of Transylvania, while other pairs glide farther
south to Lake Scutari then turn east, flying over a stony jumble of

peaks to Sofia at the foot of the Balkan Range and over these
to the country around Bucharest, gliding high over steep
forested banks of Danube as it roils and dashes through the
acute bends of the Iron Gates' deep gorges, widening in

its last stretch to its reedy, waterfowl-rich delta on the Black Sea
near Constanta; a scattered few of these great birds continuing
on a south-east diagonal, finally circling high over the
banks of the Bosphorus and Istanbul's minarets and domes.

Darker Imperial Eagles are sentinel above easterly
territory extending from north Hungary into foothills of the
Tatra Mountains, rolling landscapes around Cracow and
into Galicia, old Ruthenia and the Carpathians,

some of the birds nesting and watching over landscapes farther
east in Moldavia, then across the Prut to Kishinev and
farther north to country around Berdichev, in Volhynia,
over to ancient Kiev of the golden cupolas on the

Dnieper, some of the birds soaring still farther east on their
outspread, seeming level wings to Kharkov and beyond to the
Don, following to its delta on the Sea of Azov near
Rostov, then flying farther east still, some cross the wide Volga,

traveling down its banks as the currents roll southward, stately,
inexorable, to the Caspian Sea; farther south, other
Imperial Eagles glide over the Crimean Peninsula,
and windings of the Dnieper and Deniester to the Black Sea,

the first draining into its delta near Kerson, the second not far
from Odessa – while a few eagles range farther southwest, gliding,
watchful, above lower elevations of Balkan and Thracian mountains
to country around the Sea of Marmara and the Bosphorus.

The Eagles Clash & Fall

A sultry day in the first week of August 1914 . . . both
Golden and Imperial Eagles open great wings, disturbed by
electricity in the air, flapping pinions and lifting from perches
to rise on warm, ion-charged thermals high into air over

their territories, the Golden on wings upswept from body,
the Imperial moving on near rigid, almost level wings . . .
outspan, the huge wings of both clans show black against gathering
heaps of bruised storm-omen cumulus, while occasional rays striking

through cloud rents silhouette the birds in sun bursts of brilliant back light
as they soar, turning heads to monitor their territories with
piercing, implacable dark eyes . . . more and more of the birds
>   assemble,
>   circling, gliding, their keening cries
>   cutting the thick, charged atmosphere.

The great Golden Eagles mass over
lands from the cold Baltic down through old Rus to the Black Sea and
    above
the rock and snow-spined alps between, the birds watching Baltic waves
    change to
steel-gray chop, ruffled white caps atop, and the shallower waters of
Lake Ilmen, the Masurian Lakes, Pripet Marshes, Neusiedler See,

Lake Balaton turn tarnished pewter, dimples white-tipped in wind gusts,
while the rivers of these lands, from Oder, Vistula and mighty Danube
to smallest streams darken deep Prussian blue, ebon-shaded at banks,
their currents reflecting glints of polished sterling and opaque graphite.

Congregating Imperial Eagles
view wind fluttering birch leaves to alternating silver and jade in
hundreds of woodland groves as needles on thousands of firs and
pines sway and clash, filling air with resin scent as the steppe grains and
grasses rub and hush, stalks bending low, rising again in pale and

dark gold waves as wind rushes through, while all the flowing rivers and
the Dardanelles, Sea of Marmara, Black, Azov, Caspian seas
change from bright indigo where sun rays strike to dark sapphire
then an almost carbon-gray as the clouds increase, darken, advance.

As the sun moves east to west over these lands, in late afternoon
eagle eyes discern occasional shafts breaking through clouds, striking
sparks from gold domed churches on bluffs above wide eastern rivers
and winking off gilded weathervanes atop sharp-angled spires

in high alpine valleys, then as clouds increase and blacken, shadowing
earth, tiny lights begin twinkling far below in the habitats of
men: candle and lantern-oil light in hamlets on forest edges,
along the Pale of Settlement, in villages and towns in foothills, plains,

along rivers, lakes and sea shores, while chandeliers and gas lights glitter more brightly in linked chains and bracelets of twinkling fire in the great cities: Danzig, Riga, Saint Petersburg, Warsaw, Cracow,
    Vienna, Prague, Budapest, Trieste, Belgrade, Sofia, Moscow,
            Kiev, Odessa, Constantinople.

In this early twilight, the swirling, tremendously heaped indigo-purple cumulus in Central and East European skies seem to arrest for breathless seconds as battalions of the two largest Eagle kindred muster in agitated convocations above

places where their territories overlap . . . lines colliding, Golden and Imperial Eagles clash, smash in furious battle over Neusiedler See and Lake Balaton, tangled Balkan, Carpathian, Transylvanian Mountains, Rhodope chain, Mount Athos and ancient
   Thrace,

the Sea of Marmara, Bosphorus and Black Sea, stooping on each other, talons extended, sharp curved beaks wide in defiant screams. Primaries, secondaries, tail feathers bend, break and tear away, downy breast feathers fill the air – a Golden Eagle has eye

blinded by slashing claw, an Imperial, fatally wounded, keens then plummets into the ebon sea – as darkness grows the birds continue to fight – some, wings partly functioning, spiral to earth where they drag pinions, unable to fly – others strike ground hard

and instantly perish – many, both dead and wounded, plummet into lakes, rivers, straits . . . a red-orange sun disk, sinking below western horizon, shows briefly beneath palled black clouds, its streaming, blood-scarlet rays revealing the Imperial Eagles

entirely gone from the sky . . . one Golden Eagle, feathers ragged, remains in the air, rising laboriously upward so high it comes into clear sunlight above the clouds where it flaps slowly, heavily away, turning into a black speck against the pale gold light then dissolves into distance. The last scarlet shaft sliding under clouds dims, disappears with the sinking sun – all sky light is extinguished, and storm-black night covers Russia, Poland, Moldavia, Rumania, Serbia, Bulgaria, Macedonia, Hungary, Austria, North Italy

    and begins stretching long talons and shadow wings
        over Germany to Switzerland, Alsace, France
            unto continent's end
       in the shelving, sinking Belgian sands.

Coda

The concerto's spaciously scaled river of sound flows forward, horns voicing a haunting melody of longing while under pulsing orchestral notes the piano carries a lyric burden of aching yearning . . . a dialogue develops between orchestra and piano, and then tympani

clash in prophetic echoes of great battles, long foretold, soon to drench, even drown, hills, fields, forests, moors, marshes, stream banks,
   villages, towns,
in flowing rivers of crimson and scarlet . . . a wistful melody lulls and trills, but beneath, an underlying, growling menace from

massed instruments increases, sweeping melody away in a maelstrom of sound – until finale's trumpeting over-arching motif conquerors chaos, offers hope of clouds parting and sun one day shining on contested lands once more . . . but triumphant as this

conclusion, even at resolution's peak, hid within its heart as miniscule grain in oyster shell, is consciousness of welling sadness – awareness that the first exquisite theme is always disappearing from us, accompanied by soul-deep longing for its

return, and as the piano's crystal-cut notes continue, arrives sensation of a million steel lance and saber points pricking, stabbing fragile skin with sharp perception of the lives, landscapes, buildings, art and beauty lost in the Great War's five-year shattering of the Old World

and near-complete destruction of its fragile, iced wedding-cake construct,
the entire complex edifice disintegrating
almost instantaneously behind a tear-veiled scrim
and receding with every intervening
minute, hour, month, year
farther from our candle-flickering memories.

note: After writing the final verse, I realized it carried an echo of an Evelyn Waugh observation about how his generation mostly ignored Europe to travel to other places on the globe perceived as more exotic: 'Had we known, we might have lingered . . . had we known that all that seeming-solid, patiently built, gorgeously-ornamented structure of Western life was to melt overnight like an ice castle.' Patrick Leigh Fermor's long walk from Rotterdam to Constantinople in 1933 was the brilliant exception.

The Orient Express – Exile and Escape
1935 & 1939

Autumn across Europe – a cool northeast breeze stirs branches on ash,
 beech, oak,
linden and sycamore trees, their brittle leaves falling in legions of
hundreds and thousands to swirl and skitter over wood shingle, red tile,

copper-green roofs, spear sharp steeples, ribbed and inlaid domes, towers and
 pointed
turrets of castles perched above narrow ravines, celadon rivers . . .
one harvest season sweeps swiftly into the next on planet's restless

current of days, minutes brimming fast to hours that spill into weeks
eternally slipping from us to disappear in the flooding rush of years
blossoming, fruiting, dropping brittle leaves between the present and

September of Thirty-Five when Herr Professor Erich Auerbach took
his considered departure for fabled Constantinople, boarding
the Paris Orient-Express at Munich – two-faced city divided

perpetually between twin-towered Frauenkirche on the gracious
Marienplatz, and the Wiesn meadow where every September since
1810's royal wedding, beer halls roar to rowdy Breughel-esque life.

Out of the city, a landscape cultivated for centuries glides past
Herr Auerbach: fields edged in thickets frost-burnt topaz and ruby,
timber and white-wash hamlets and farmhouses, villas in parkscapes.

The Professor, though more displaced with every mile carrying him farther
from familiar libraries and dictionaries, desk and chair, is always and
foremost preoccupied with comparisons burgeoning in his head,

and so well-entrenched in his specific discipline – the painstaking
analysis of language poets have employed through the span of western
civilization to show forth reality – that even in his current

circumstance the parade of scenes slipping past a window would, perhaps,
seem no more manifestation of the real than images wavering
by in rarely-viewed newsreels. A glance out before he opens one of his

last moment tucked-in-valise journals presents eye-filling picture of
sky-slicing gray-blue mountain ramparts, slim white church spire dazzling
  against
dense fir slopes cut by meadows dotted with trim chalets displaying far and

nearer tiny figures of shepherds, grazing goats, cows. Later, double- steeple
pilgrimage church on green-gold hill above the Danube signals Linz as track
continues along storied river for miles of clackety-clack, passing

terraced vineyards, neat villages, gold-brown hazel, oak and beech woods
  fringed with
pale-stemmed birches, their crisped gilt leaves flickering and dancing in
  winking sunlight;
a bend, and with startling abruptness, St Stefan's gaudy roof and substantial

late Gothic spire rise from the bronze-topaze tree canopy and green-
patina copper domes of royal Hapsburgs' ringed city; soon after,
glancing up from article absorbing him, the Professor registers in

certain bemusement wavering cursive lines of storks, ducks, geese migrating
above Danube's tree-stitched plain patchworked in ochre pumpkins, rye and
  new-sown
winter wheat. A short sprint east ends in right angle curve to bridge-linked
  Buda-Pest,

and here the Professor's train – route impulse chosen by
scholar's appreciation of Roumania's language – crosses Danube to
begin the long southeast slant toward Bucharest; different journal

in another of his eight languages now engaging him, the crossing of
Hungary's stretched-to-horizon pustza – vast sweeps of grain and feather
  grasses
scattered with huge flocks of sheep, mounted herders, occasional low
  homesteads

beneath clustered trees near long-arm well pole – is ignored by the professor,
who doesn't glance up until the train, slowing, begins its snaking switchback
into the Carpathian Alps. Morning finds our passenger, after

breaking his fast in dining car with rolls and life-reviving
coffee, passing spectacular views of scarp and lake, forest and granite
peak, but now he's jotting notes for scholarly rebuttal of article

read day before, missing sight of white and pearl gray doves flying above
an ochre-washed Saxon fortress-church, dark firs massed behind, in
   Transylvania's
craggy Siebenburgen, the birds' fluttering wings, translucent in rising sun

diffusing glinting gold-dust over the complex of red roofs within the thick
outer wall. Round every curve now, fleeting glimpses of spiky castles
atop sword-sharp cliffs and fairytale Pied Piper towns – turreted gate-houses,

shadowed archways, cobble streets, curlicue fountains in quaint squares,
   gables and
dormers peeping over jumbled roof-scapes – until the train, constantly
   braking,
begins gradual descent, slithering down steep gradients and across high

arcing spider-web bridges. The audible gasps of passengers peering
into heart-stopping declivities cause even the contained Professor
to put aside his reading and stare down one knife-sliced gorge to a river

frothing hundreds of feet below – and surprise himself experiencing
several breath-caught seconds. On the train winds, beside precipitous ravines
and up-thrusting rock palisades, along twisty fir and pine slopes, in and out

dim tunnels before, with a sigh of escaping steam, achieving lower ground;
picking up speed through poplar-edged mud brown fields and drab one-
   street villages,
the train slips past Polest's oil derricks raising strangely prehistoric

skeletons against the eastern sky, and rolls into Bucharest, Second
Empire Hausmann boulevards, ponderous Wilhelmine Imperial
buildings sprouting amidst the districts of disheveled peasant shtetls

that mushroomed inside a medieval fortress. Another climb carries train
   over
wildcat crouched, shoulder-hunched Balkan Mountains to reach Turkey's
   border at
Adrianople; following soon after, the domes and minarets of the

chaos-incarnate megalopolis on the Bosporus where Herr
Auerbach, clutching precious valise, disembarks in the echoing high,
glass roof station, walking exhausted but upright into his exile's life.

Contrasting this correspondence-arranged exit of the Professor from
his congenial university position (congenial until the
bludgeoning escalation of edicts against Jews) – some four years later,

another traveler sets off on the Orient Express, Simplon line. In
March of the slow-detonating land-mine year of Thirty-Nine, Miss Freya
Stark, committed traveler with a poet's passionate soul and instant

response to the world beyond her skin, makes a precipitate escape
combining flight from the clogging mundane with her quest to encounter
   life
in places where existence a more urgent, stripped-to-bone affair than

the padded-cushion life on offer those years for Europe's privileged classes.
Her books scintillate with lightning-strike insights, at times wrong-headed,
   more
often illuminating, in a style as far from the Professor's measured

conclusions as possible to find. Miss Stark, after a day of meeting
friends and dining in St Mark's water-girdled city – hats and white
gloves for the ladies – sets off in the morning from Venice station, crossing

the mist-blue Friulian plain in that state of exhilaration she
always experiences fleeing the comfortable groove of the familiar.
At the top of the indigo Adriatic, melancholy Trieste

achieved, the stones of civic buildings and port weighted with memories of
Austria's lost monarchy; rounding peninsula's corner, the view north
is spring greening meadows and woods below Julian Alps gray-silver wall,

while the next stretch south looks on fresh ploughed fields, orchards, tidy
  villages all
the way to Zagreb on the blue Sava – cream and yellow washed stucco
  facades,
red roofs and twin cathedral spires palimpsest for twice twenty provincial

capitals in Franz-Joseph's once-upon-a-time Empire. Into
Serbia a more improvised landscape begins – huts and tumbledown shacks
  huddled
beneath spreading willows, horses in lush pastures racing the train, manes
  and tails

streaming, country lanes empty save for plodding peasant, donkey and cart,
  small
girl driving geese all arrow dream swift past Miss Stark's window till at
  confluence
Danube and Sava, blood-drenched Belgrade reached, spilling beyond its
  founding

fortress promontory, unstable for centuries with a gelignite mix
of Greek Orthodox, Catholic, and Muslim; farther south, mountain
  surrounded
Nish, Constantine's birth city, marking gateway route connecting east and
  west

from ancient days; soon after, valley between low hills conjures
Sophia's slim minarets lifting above hovels and sheds, with
glimpses of rock outcrops and fir-crested spine of the Balkan range;

later Miss Stark's glance surveys the succession of shabby wood stations
where kerchief'd women in crow black wait beside baskets and bundles,
sharp eyes in seamed faces watching the Express flash past. At last,

Adrianople's worn platform with the gypsy band, and soon after
journey's end in Istanbul's cacophonous, arcade-pillared,
bubble-domed, mosaic-tiled, minaret-towered Byzantine confusion.

Miss Stark, journeying on, will take the Taurus Express
down the Coast of Incense, her slight figure vanishing in mid-East
   landscapes

and war years' Foreign Office intelligence work before return to Tuscan
hill town sanctuary; Herr Professor Auerbach, tucked in his Istanbul

academic bunker, writes his seminal work between Forty-Two and
Forty-Five, at war's end emigrating to U.S.A., though longing

always for his homeland – yet when his old position at Marburg
University offered, he refuses, dying in exile not long after. . . .

Two travelers: both sensing their world's disintegration, both attempting
to preserve remembrance of ways of living and thinking fast disappearing

even before the war – one by use of surgeon-precise line by line
language dissection, the other by swift visceral response to crumbling

monuments, scarred artifacts . . . but time's irresistible, outgoing tide
carries the worlds they wrote of farther from us every second, while no
   means

exists to recover or repair the millions of prismed crystal globes
dropped and shattered in the vertiginous chasm of those dark decades.

         Only fragmented shards of memory –
    a drifting cloud of gritty, pulverized carbon that glows
      phosphor green-black in our fading earth light –
        survive to prick, and occasionally stab,
          our pale and strengthless hands.

Temple on Headland

*Figures in a Dream,
Voices on the Wind*

Danaë

Leaning from window in her brazen tower, wrapped in winter's white
wool, gold-fringed chiton, she waits, bones a-jangle with repressed motion,
through the dragging seconds, minutes, hours of her prisonment. . . .

This day, a thick storm cloud potent with rain moves from out the north
toward distant sea and Cycladic archipelago, obscuring
islands, water . . . pressure begins throbbing in her temples and

heaviness weighs her limbs . . . overcome by dizzied faintness she moves
to her couch, seeking relief of smooth linen, but finds instead
the heated swelling of her flesh increases to such a shuddering

fever she tears cloth away to lie naked, legs a-sprawl. Turning
head, she watches roiling thunder-murk push between the window's
columns, smoking obsidian cloud edges transforming to blazing gilt,

and as the Divine Wind and Rain gust inside the chamber, hovering
above the supine woman, the light-rimmed clouds begin
raining fat drops of liquid gold, the incandescence touching face,

neck, shoulders, hips, arms, legs – enveloping her entire being in
a moist aether of pulsing warmth that dilates veins and tissues in
stomach, breasts, thighs, groin, nipples, labia, softening every inch of

skin and setting her a-tremble with desire. Compelled in each blood
cell, her legs open wide to receive the fountaining, jetting stream of
heated gold liquescence thrusting, penetrating to her deepest, inmost core.

On becoming receptacle of Great Zeus's molten spill, Danaë waits,
patient, fulfilled, upon her child's hour despite trials attending such a
genesis and knowledge of prophecy: this boy will be Perseus,
fate-destined slayer of Acrisius, king of Argos, his grandfather.

Three Winds

A woman rests on stone bench of pillar-enclosed
courtyard in spring, hands clasped on lap of white robe . . .

Boreas gusts cool breaths from the north, tearing
petals from blossoming plums, scattering them

across paving stones and shallow pool where they
form broken pink mosaics on the rippled

surface . . . a goldfinch flutters from branch to
branch, pecking buds, brushed enamel gold-gilt wing bands

flashing – a sword slices white lightning across
the woman's mind . . . never will he bide next

to her again and share some transient joy:
color of a bird's wing – rising sun's slow spill
of pale honey over sharp limestone crags.

A summer night – the woman descends steep steps,
sits on marble terrace balustrade . . . Notus

puffs soft south breezes across gentle sea swells,
diffuses twining jasmine's scent, sets thin pine

needle shadows trembling in the ghost light
cast from a silver-white moon ship rocking west

whiles glowing, spray-plumed star clouds swirl mystic
calligraphies across an ebon firmament . . .

he has left – gone so distant far if she
sailed leagues across vast oceans, and walked

earth's pathways years through desert, forest and
mountain till feet bled and hair greyed, still she
would not arrive the faint track to his dwelling.

One gold-infused autumn blue afternoon,
the woman meditates on crumbling cliff top

near sheer, heart-stopping drop . . . wind gods jostle and
contest from every quarter, contrary airs

ruffling waves below – to, fro, crosswise on
water the same dark blue his eyes . . . if she stands,

easy to let the unchancy winds blow her
where they list . . . if one pushed her to edge and

over, the lead weighing her heart's core would sink
her quick as stone – no more need she lie

wakeful and weeping, or trouble the gods with
vain plaints. She rises, paces back, turns, faces

west – abruptly the wind veers, Eurus pressing strong
from the east against her spine . . . she moves forward –

fast, faster – runs straight into air over
the sea . . . as her body plummets, her head fills
with an enormous, pulsing white-gold sun –

        bursting,
    its radiance instantly winks out.

Beyond the Well at the World's End

Certain nights, beneath a waning gibbous moon's crepuscular light,
a woman's thin shivering shape stands beside the well at world's end,

thirsting – pale hands wind bucket down, bring it back, dip metal cup . . .
choking on thick, bitter brine that burns mouth and gorge, she lifts eyes to

alien landscape – prickly knotgrass threads creeping around spiky
sword grass clumps, tall, serrate-edge succulents, twisted thorn shrubs, and

shadow-sliced swales strewn with glinting, glass-sharp obsidian chips.
Dropping cup, she moves across dry ditches to serried sand hills

rising and falling in bleached waves to stone shingle fringing a vast
murk-black ocean where great sea dragons raise reptile heads as they plunge

through oleose billows that surge and subside in hushing swells toward
a far horizon obscured by dense wove, ebon velvet curtain

fitfully illumined by knife-edge bolts of yellow-white-green
actinic lightning. Often when the humpback moon seems to bend its

sad clown face lower, tear drop spilling from cratered eye, she searches
sky for stars, but in the wan ghost light never finds minutest

silver-bright dart; other times she stoops, dabbles fingers in water,
touches tongue and tastes sea flavor familiar as her own veins' scarlet

blood . . . always, though, she wakes to sliding salt tears, the caustic crystals
clogging lashes, crusting lips – and fresh red splotching white pillow.

Long years later, wavering steps return the woman to world's last
well and sand barrens beyond to shingle shore . . . she wades through warm

swell to empty skiff wave-bobbed toward her, clambers in, hoists sail –
that instant, a keening small wind from the northeast billows the sail,

pushes boat out . . . murk-gray days on the sullen sea blur to moonless
nights when water lit by teeming rafts of translucent corpse-glow

jellyfish and ringed sea worms squirming, swirling so dense entwined
even the sagging clouds tainted with their phosphor luster. The skiff

sways on for countless leagues, its sail wearing to gauze threads, the woman
near to perishing of thirst, flesh shrinking to brittle bone till, at

penultimate, hope-lost moment, a streak of incandescent
platinum slashes through weighted atmosphere, instantly sundering

dark-piled clouds to the south – a royal indigo sky banner
unfurls where fantastic, air-spun mirage shimmers: beyond wave

ruffled shore, a shining, towered city rises, its spired, arched,
ivory fretwork palaces, minarets, gilded domes gleaming

above massive white walls, palms and orange trees stirring in a soft
wind that wafts essences of cinnamon, clove, jessamine and rose

over sapphire water scattered with scintillant treasure of sun-gold
sequins. A dappled horse races along the yellow sand, ridden by one

robed, turbaned in immaculate white, jeweled khanjar hilt glittering
in the citron light . . . the rider turns his steed, splashes into the

surf, leans down, blue eyes glinting, tanned face breaking into the smile that
broke her heart a thousand thousand times, and he gathers her close

with sinew-strong arms. Arrived at last in her weary heart's safe
       haven, the woman sighs, softer than breath . . .
              her eyelids flutter . . . and close.

Two Figures in Moonlight
sketch after a lost Caspar David Friedrich painting

May midnight – a full moon veiled by thin cloud haze.
Two figures stand by a dark mere, its mirror

surface shivering from least air breath that fragments
moon's reflected orb into silvery splinters

and wanders, sighing, through serried ranks of fringing
reeds. A hidden, black-crowned heron voices three harsh
        staccato calls then falls silent.

A raised, flat-topped rock – the woman sits, gathering
summer weave cloak close – the man's hand comes down, grips

her shoulder hard, pressing into bone. All that is
imagined of heart-shaking desire joined with shared

laughter to ward against parting's approaching
shadow has already passed between these two . . .

one star-blazed night in their canopied bed, a child
has been seeded . . . this dawn he leaves on service sworn

an Alamann king, leaving her torn asunder
before the birth, and him forever riding
        away from his heart's desire.

The Faery Lover

In a fair country – poplar bordered vales, silver
birches swaying in daisied meads and hollows,

domed, pillared shrines atop pillow blue hills, bright
fountains hid in dusky dells – a perfect faery

lover once came to me, slim, tall, ivory pale,
night-wing black hair, clear eyes cold as starlight. 'Neath

fluttering, unfurling beech canopy of
tender, green-gold leaves and clustered tree blossoms

dropping sweetness over us we kissed, clasped,
caressed, then pressing me down on the bluebells, he

fondled my smooth white breasts, and with clever
fingers teased and tortured until my soft, moist

layers unfolded as a rose its morning
petals and I moaned for surcease. Whence he parted

my resistless thighs, plunging his thickened sword deep
in my honeyed sheath, and we fused, clinging each to

each on the crushed bluebells under the spreading beech,
lengthily pleasuring to climax each from the

other in the perfect consummation that
dissolves the bounds of separate selves. But at last the

godhead shrunk, withdrew, my inward-outward waves
of shuddering tremblings ceased and sweet juices dried. . . .

The beech leaves now hang brittle, frost-burnt and withered,
while I have lain for days and cried in the brown deadfall

under the trees – and wisht then had died, not found, dragged
back, flesh seen bit and bruised through rent gown, and ever

after pointed, whispered as lackwit victim duped
by malicious nymphs weaving their gossamer-webbed,

sticky-clinging ensorcellings to beguile chill
winter's tedium with lascivious midsummer dreams.

The Forest Glade

I wait in the forest glade beneath silver shimmering
birches for the one I chose, and shudder, thinking of

that other – hatchet face, grim slash of mouth, narrowed eyes
assessing, stripping me bare at contract signing then quickly

discarding my body as wanting (more to his taste
the full-breasted serving wenches – tumbled red and brown curls,

plump haunches swelling beneath kilted skirts – rather than
this reed slender shape and fall of platinum hair, pale as rain).

They are so busy scurrying here and there readying
the marriage feast for once I am less close watched – none

spied the arrow-swift, secret glances that passed between me
and new-hired minstrel . . . my old nurse messenger, two

brief meetings, of grace, contrived – yesternoon after sext, and
now these last shining, god-gifted moments before vespers . . .
      I have not been granted right to ask more.

Tomorrow, after I am wed, and the feasting, this man
my guardians dowered with my great heritance will

rape me through the long night (nurse and I contriving with dried
blood on small sea sponge inside me to stain sheets), then

mount, batter me again whenever his urgent lust to get
an heir burns hot – and after one is birthed, he will require

another, then another, till between two and three or
four the birth certain to go awry: babe turned wrong in

my womb or miscarried and fever raging . . . as I go
out on a tide of warm red blood, I hope to see again

this trembling-leaved, cool green glade, the minstrel with his grave
half-smile, body straight and whip-pliant as a young birch, and

recall the keen blade of white-gold ardor that flared between
us as he played so nimbly on limbs that never again will

know hope or desire, only stone cold duty until
at last released into skeleton death's chill embrace.

Summer grasses rustle with his light step – he is here, crisp
auburn locks, clean young scent and long clever fingers that will

stroke, tease, coax my body to sing as a Cymru lyre. . . .
This memory I will carry under my breastbone always –

down grey days and black nights to the flame-shot darkness of my
appointed end . . . which every morn I will pray sweet Lady
Mary, Mother of God, to allow of her mercy come soon.

 I wish the birch trees wept their silver-green leaves over
   our two corpses, stone-dead, entwined.

The Courtly Lover
Stanzas in the Jacobean Manner

Once, when Lady Spring – prism-winged, inconstant nymph
and wanton – spread her gemmed train over copses and
woods, making swell myriad buds in lustered pearl shades

on tree and shrub – tossing, careless, her dew-spangled
green girdle to earth in south-slant hollows – opening
her flowered gowan in sheltered vales and hedged

meadows – stirring with balmy perfumed breath violets,
daisies, primroses awake – and wrapt only in
transparent rainbow gauzes disported above,

arcing her perfect form whiles fertilizing showers
bedewed the receptive loam, I – eyes bedazzled by
such shining pageant – first envisioned love the moment

you captured its glossy, mirrored image in my
swiftly beglamoured mind, reflecting that treacherous
emotion back to me as I wished it to see.

Thus become a fool fondly fancying love returned,
I bloomed forth with the unrestrained, tumescent season,
donning silken robes of emeraud and amethyst

broidered in white marguerite, gilt buttercup, pink
campion and blue bell for secret dalliance in
hidden, grass-velvet dells, you first fingering lute

and singing honeyed wooing rhymes, then soon after
beginning a nimbler strumming on my limbs, playing
between lips and breasts before shifting key to lower,

deeper mode between my thighs until I opened
heedlessly to you as tender, thoughtless buds
to Zephyrus's April soft caresses.

But on hill tops and in shade-deep ravines, skeleton
Winter still clasped Gaea in his cold embrace, and
that May white-haired Boreas sent sudden ice-storm

from his chill north realm, blighting, shriveling in
instants the incautious blossoms as did my love
for you when I, passing tapestry-hung arras and

discerning cloth's strange movement, twitched it aside
to see your bare haunches thrusting hard between
the thick splayed legs of a fat scullery wench.

Black Horse at Sunset

Twilight – a white track winds high across wine-stained heath,
sole traveler a cloaked, hooded figure carrying
a rush basket, walking fast. Now and again

the maiden casts a quick glance back, face in the dusk
glimmer pale. Shifting burden, she runs and stumbles
down incline between steep slopes to ways' meet, then stops,

flight-poised, at milestone. The last stretch – hope leaps heart –
but as she pauses, scant-breathed, she feels from ground through
feet and bones faintest throbbing vibration of hooves.

She stands statue-frozen until her ears begin to
hear sound pounding nearer, and out of a flame lurid
west Devon sunset a rider on a night black steed

crests the ridge behind. At last she turns, flees, but hills,
gullies empty of aid and the horse veers beside her,
hard-pulled to rear against cerise-streaked amethyst sky.

The girl cries out, whirls, hood falling away to reveal
tresses enmeshing sunset's embers curling, rippling
in fire-gold splendor about her head, down her back.

The black-avised brigand laughs – flash of white, sharp teeth –
reaches down and with an iron grip drags the girl
onto the horse. The basket drops, spills packets – flour,

tea, skein of crimson yarn – onto the path. Quick jabs
of sharp-roweled spurs, and the horse races toward the
darkness advancing from the empurpled, cloud-piled east.

November Storm - Merioneth

Warm west wind – autumn in Wales and on this ocean's
remote Pacific Northwest coast: here light shafts and

slants much the same as there, bruised cobalt-gray clouds pile
and tumble in shifting winds while raindrops spatter,

heralding storm . . . abrupt, a scene imposes – angled
mind, mirror-tilted, capturing in silvered brilliance

   clear reflection of a long-lost memory. . . .

Backed by lush pastures and hunched, worn grey mountains,
white-washed, slate-roof cottages face across shore road

to Cardigan Bay, where in the cool, rinsed morning
after a wild, high tide November storm, a woman –

strong breezes fluttering long black skirt, checked shawl pulled
over head and shoulders – stands above slick, dark rocks

watching white-crested marine-green waves thundering
landward to crash over breakwater in foaming

gouts while amongst tattered, fleeing cloud legions of
marbled amethyst and indigo, a heart-lifting,

heaven-transparent aquamarine reveals for
sun-dazzled seconds, vanishes, then briefly shines

again on slick rocks, rain-filled hollows . . . instead of
glistening, prisoned, from black, trash-littered asphalt

and reflecting in sheet glass skyscraper facades
in a city where a girl – short skirt, high boots – at

bus-stop turns her face up to pricking raindrops as
instant's glimpse behind centuries' curtaining folds

of a place half a world away disappears, leaving
only the piercing keens of herring gulls riding Welsh

wind gusts echoing down fast-funneled sand glass years to
repeat in cries of white-gray glaucous gulls spiraling

against dark clouds over the mini-skirted girl's head.

Path of the Summer Stars

Beyond the nights of wild weeping arrive hopeless
dawns and the slow seep of tears into a pillow. . . .

A woman sits above rock-bound cove indented on
the knife-edge of Ocean's desolation, beneath an

overarching immensity of black, where thick star
clouds revolve and Aquila's sparkling constellation,

swooping west, sheds silver-gilt slivers, feather curved,
atop sea swells, lumining narrow path shimmering

to the horizon. Behind the woman, a faint track
winds through dry grasses and clumps of thrift; before her,

tide's retreat has drawn out the sea, exposing a long
slope of glistening sand – a sharp scent of salt and pine

resin tingles in the air. Time passes . . . abruptly
the woman stands, clambers down rocks and walks slowly

forward beneath the pulsing stars. As she moves, Ocean's
insistent growl increases and sand underfoot

vibrates with the pounding beat of a turning tide . . .
as Ocean returns, springing, surging toward the woman,

she resolves to fling herself within opening maw
of first wave to crest overhead – its crushing weight will

batter her and child in her belly to pulp – with bare
chance Fate-sent second billow might lift her instead

on white spume stair to Ocean's high-ridged, rippling spine . . .
there she will follow path of broken star tiles across

the desolate water waste, the silver glinting
crescents guiding her to shore in a distant land where

unknown planets quietly glimmer above velvet
folded hills and shadowed meadows. . . . The wave crashes

over her, smashing, blinding, deafening – briefly
she is lifted – glimpses bright Aquila plunging

into Ocean, star-bright breast feathers extinguishing . . .
the silver-gilt pathway trembles . . . shortens . . . disappears.

Alpine Triad – Fragments

Sudden glimpsed line – a curved, high arc of green hill
swelling against rinsed azure sky – wakes again that
heart-deep ache to walk away one spring morning, climb

steep path up alp to plateau where cloud shadows sweep
across deer nibbled turf, then lie back, at peace,
beneath a clear, tinkling waterfall of lark song.

Rushing down jagged rock-strewn slopes, warm east wind
soughs airy oceans through fir and pine boughs, swirls
cool breaths of spicy resin through wood, plaster and

whitewash village, rustles leaves on lindens around
fountain square and twirls the gilt stag-above-arrow
weathervane atop church spire into a blurred spin.

A maiden – hair in braided coronet, patched gown
and embroidered apron – follows track through brambles to
fir-circled glade . . . placing pinecone filled basket by

mossed rock, she sits, contemplates a solitary,
gray-trunked beech grown tall on low mound, its autumn leaves
lighting a golden torch in the forest's dark heart.

Waxwings
for Ruth

Warm resin-scented August air tingles with trilling calls
and continual blurred burry-buzzes of waxwings
conversing in cedars and pines. One fine fellow – dark mask,

buff crest, yellow paint dipped tail tip, secondaries splashed in
blood-red sealing wax drips – preens and stretches wings on scarlet
berried rowan branch set against whipped cream piles of tumbling,

building cloud castles in a summer sky of clean-washed, stainless
blue. Bird, branch and white clouds most properly create foreground
and background of illustration to some tale collected by

Jacob or Wilhelm Grimm, now lost. . . . In front of cloud
pinnacles, this painted scene would depict needle sharp peaks
and steep pastures where goats roam and tiny chalets perch, a

walled gray-stone castle in distance – capped battlements, jutting
turrets, roofed towers, snapping dragon-tongue banners – frowning
atop stark cliff lifted above leagues of dark, thick-pelt firs

stitched with lighter patches – ash, birch, hawthorn, hazel, linden,
oak and sycamore. Beneath the forest canopy
ragged woodcutters chop, wicked robbers prowl, malicious

sorcerers and hump-back witches plot, antlered stags run before
silver hunting horns, boars stand at bay before spears, and
bear, wildcat, wolf lurk in bramble-tangled undergrowth.

The forgotten tale* might tell of young maid clothed in patches
and wise innocence setting off from alpine hut, basket on
arm, to pick blackberries one blue sky summer morning,

continue with her stopping to gather three feathers dropped by
waxwings – her favorite bird – go on with disguised prince riding
out of forest and meeting the maiden, and after diverse

singular incidents, recount adventure in which feathers
prove the charm that breaks spell holding prince captive in wizard's
dank dungeon, then relate dangerous escape and more trials

before rightful end attained: moment at spousal feast when
staunch maid – gowned now in blue silk – has prince's grateful father
place on her head a crown of glinting gold and sapphires

centered with talisman waxwing feathers, gilt-dipped, with
affixed to middle one's tip by master goldsmith's art,
a trembling ruby teardrop pulsing heart's blood scarlet.

---

* *note:* This story, with many others from lost centuries, swirl within Father Time's clouded scrying glass. A present-day collector in the tradition of the Brothers Grimm has spent long years peering into this star-dusted glass, retrieving therefrom a number of fascinating fragments.

Presently the tale concerning the waxwings' talisman is being meticulously transcribed. The complete version of this adventure with all details pertaining thereunto concerning maiden and prince, dastardly spell, witch, sorcerer, perilous escape using the three feathers, and What Occurred After will, the editor hopes, soon be writ out complete for readers to peruse, along with diverse other stories new-discovered by the compiler.

Biedermeier Autumn
Beethoven String Quartet No.15, 1825

Wide, gray satin river slides through valley
beneath steep snow-shrouded peaks submerging
under billows of indigo-purple cloud.
Gold-leaved alders and willows fringe water's edge

path where girl in headscarf walks toward clustered
white-washed houses, steep pitched roofs huddled
round gilt-tipped needle slim spire set in
plaited fields of brown, dark amber, olivine.

Fierce-fanged fortress crouches atop gray crag
lifting from beech and fir forest where curl
of ghost-gossamer smoke rises from trees
into dusk's blue chill while red-gold fire,

glinting down aisle of silver-gray trunks, shows
shadows leaping, spinning to fiddle strings' wild
sobs and fast glissandos as the first white
star pricks silver stitches in darkening sky.

Proud perched Benedictine abbey crowns rock
prow cleaving swift Danube's strong current. Sun
reflecting off ochre walls releases ripe,
honey-spiced scents – apple, plum, pear, quince – to

waft down steep vine-clad slopes where men and
women heap giant wicker baskets with
translucent clusters of gem-bright ruby,
garnet, peridot, amethyst treasure.

Woven in music's elusive spell, these
diaphanous, trembling webs limn texture, tint,
movement . . . but the quartet notes, forward compelled,
scatter fast as windblown and swirled autumn leaves,

intruding shivering breath of cold future
into these air-spun fancies . . . clouds begin
spitting rain, hurrying girl along track – leaves
whirl in icy gust and ragged gypsies drop,

crouch by dying flames – bent harvesters stand, heft
laden baskets . . . each successive melodic
phrase thins the glimpsed visions, fading the jewel
colors to glass transparence until by last

chords they are entirely dissolved into
nothingness, save for faintest sighing, tingling
vibration of atoms that scarcely disturbs
        surrounding atmosphere.

Souvenir of Old Provence

Glazunov, *Les Saisons,* premiered Mariinsky Theatre, 1900

Honeyed melody winds brazen trumpets
through autumn's cool blue, arrowing sharps to

shiver down spine, scattering crisp metallic
silver-gold clef notes across memory

of Mediterranean azure skies where
boreal winds send pine needles and leaves –

chestnut, plane, almond, red bud, fig – skittering
and tumbling across sun-bleached Roman ruins,

orange tile roofs and along the mazy paths
and ordered hillslope vine rows of old Provence.

A maiden, basket-laden, turns homeward from
the market town, ascending a curving dust-white

track through the heat-baked landscape . . . opposite
a trunk-twisted olive, she opens wicket in

wall by one of the urn-topped pillars beside
wrought-iron gates . . . down a plane tree, shade-flickered

avenue, the young woman walks into her
life within the faded ochre walls of a

green-shuttered, wisteria trellised manor-farm,
and the year's cycle of growth, harvest, decay

where, one day, they will lay her bones beneath blue
enamel sky arcing in spring above blooming

almond, cherry, peach and plum orchards, summer
fields of poppies, lavender, juniper and

thyme where lakes of tawny grain pool around
spired cypresses — and all seasons' changing

skies that curve over aisles of tall, gray-trunked
poplars transforming leaves from silver-lime to

silver-jade then burning these into autumn
spires of bronze-gold flame only quenched by

winter's rain and ice stripping the trees into
bare-limbed black etchings of themselves — until once

more budding branch tips swell mauve against clean-rinsed,
turquoise gauze to form high naves of delicate

air-pierced Gothic arches from the pliant, twig-enmeshed
       lace fretwork of another year's March.

Concert Hall Rendezvous, 1919
Rachmaninoff Piano Concert No. 2

Listening to this piece one afternoon, a mirror-bright splinter
cast from some distant, blazing star spins across ethereal
abysses a hundred black years wide, passing in an instant through

time-warped decades to suddenly strike arrow point sharp into
my dreaming mind and lodge in my startled, unprepared heart.

The young woman waits in a gas-lit, marble pillared, ivory
foyer of a concert hall . . . clutching a small beaded bag, she
glances around then back to watch the doors, rhinestone clip in piled

hair sparkling as she moves head. She pulls her long black coat – velvet rubbed
thin in places – closer. Brilliant crystal chandelier lights refract,
stabbing her eyes, splintering her vision – the crowd presses too close,

voices too loud: women in furs, décolleté satin gowns, glittering
gems in ears, round necks, men in tuxes, here and there army and
navy uniforms. The woman waiting fears a headache, frowns, as she

continues scanning doors where well-dressed folk stream through. Did he have to
work late? Perhaps cannot come at all? Tickets were expensive but
she'd prefer to leave if he can't be beside her to hear the piece.

An usher opens middle door once more – behind two dressed-to-nines
couples, a tall man in tailored olive uniform, lieutenant-
colonel silver oak leaves on shoulder tabs, overseas stripes on sleeves.

She lifts her arm . . . spotting her, he smiles, swiftly cuts path to stand
before her, 'You look like you've been worrying – you know I'd have
sent word if I couldn't make it. Have you the tickets?' She opens

bag, gives him them. 'Shall we?' His hand firm on her back he steers her
   through
crowd into auditorium, collects programs from usher, then
has her precede him to their row. In her seat, she takes arms from coat

and he helps her drape it round her shoulders . . . the orchestra files in,
the large space, a-buzz with conversation, quieting as instruments
tune; then lights dim and applause greets conductor, swells for thin, stiffly

upright man following who seats himself at the gleaming Steinway
grand. The conductor's baton drops and first notes from the orchestra
fall like doom. The uniformed man takes the woman's hand as the

concerto begins, themes singing, clashing, fading, returning, building,
accelerating to crashing conclusion that for some moments
after leaves vibrating in air the passion this superbly crafted

score and expertly played instruments called forth – a beyond-tears
evocation of a world's foredoomed end – a world now entirely
   swept away on an inexorable, blood-scarlet tide by this
      chilly February date in nineteen-nineteen.

note: Sergei Rachmaninoff emigrated with his family to America in 1918 after the Russian Revolution. He lived first in New York and made a living by playing his compositions in solo concerts and with orchestras. This poem takes place in Carnegie Hall, a favored venue for such concerts at that time. The two people in it are loosely based on my grandmother, a music-lover and terrific pianist, and my grandfather, who served in the US Army in The Great War.

Carniola, August 1943
Brahms Opus 118, Six pieces for Piano, 1893

Within a weighted atmosphere, sky heat-bleached blue,
a young woman – laced boots, black skirt, apron, head scarf

vivid with stylized folk art flowers – walks dust bisque
track between topaz wheat and rye, pale blond oat crops.

On northern horizon, pallid lilac mountains
shimmer behind low hills spilling into reed-fringed

lake; nearer, ruler straight poplar rows bisect
tawny fields, meet the path. The girl stops in the tall

trees' thin, cinerous shade, leans against a fissured
trunk, watching thunderheads build citadels over

distant alps, their livid hues alchemizing peaks
a deep amethyst, plain to anvil-hammered gold,

the poplar trunks brushed steel with black-emerald
leaves, their undersides burnished, glinting silver gilt. . . .

From noontime wireless broadcast, piano notes that
first came faint, static-sprinkled, then electric bright,

repeat again in girl's mind, this time as delayed
echo unscrolling across the leaden pall of

heaven, flashing horizon to horizon before
fading into storm-charged air where sulphurous sun rays,

slashing through advancing clouds edged in forge-molten,
thin platinum rims, cast a corpse-tainted phosphorescence

over cobalt foothills, ink green trees, burnt ochre
fields. High grasses beside the dry ditch rasp with the

clashing sound of distant swords, sharp tips spearing the
last flares of sunlight streaking down the sere bronze stems,

breaking these into a million glittering shards
seconds before rain begins lashing down and

   the girl at last turns, runs for home.

Warp and Weft

Carrying lily bouquet, a woman descends to the man waiting
on a station platform one sultry summer afternoon in
green field and hedgerow surrounded English shire town in

thirty-eight . . . far away, great thunderheads bloom over the cold
Baltic, a strong, rising wind tearing the towering clouds into
storm wings sweeping from East Prussia over Poland and north

Germany toward the Low Countries . . . 'How was town?' 'Stifling – the air was
so thick I could hardly breathe', 'We'll be home soon – always better with
all our trees – though I think a storm's coming.' Arm round her waist, he steers

her from platform to waiting car, porter pushing luggage-piled cart
behind. Decades earlier, in ought-eight, another woman,
sable-wrapped, waits beside tall, mustached man in cavalry

major's uniform, her trunks piled on train platform in Orşova,
town above the Iron Gates, awaiting the Orient Express.
'You will be able to get leave to come to Budapest in autumn,

won't you?' she asks. 'My dear, of course. These are just manoeuvers to show
those pesky Serbs our flag – quite a troop build-up across the way,' he
nods toward Danube, 'and Hötzendorf thought it wise. Nothing to worry

about.' To herself, woman thinks, 'This time.' Then whistle, headlight, black smoke
from funnel and train pulls in – brakes screech, luggage stowed, the couple kiss,
she steps up, takes seat by window, waves suede glove, is carried away.

Farther back still, in Vienna's eighteen eighty-eight winter
season, couples waltz on polished parquet floors beneath
thousands of faceted crystal chandelier drops in a constantly

shifting kaleidoscope of sparkling gems and brilliant color: diamonds,
topazes, rubies, emeralds, sapphires glitter, pink, turquoise, rose,
lilac, white satin gowns swirl and shimmer amidst black tailcoats and

red, blue, yellow, green dress uniforms stiff with medals, orders, gilt
epaulettes, emblems, tassels, braid, some with showy capes slung on gold
cords over a shoulder, all boasting swords with engraved, jeweled hilts in

a dying empire's display of encrusted, ostentatious ceremony
this last year before the first tremor of advancing cataclysm:
January eighty-nine Crown Prince Rudolf's suicide at Mayerling,

followed in ninety-eight by the first anarchist assassination –
Empress Elizabeth on a Geneva quay – true prelude to the
Balkan Wars and the madness unleashed in Sarajevo.

Always, through decades and eras, wars small and large flare for months
sometimes years, then statesmen sign treaties, peace reigns briefly before
war ignites once more – and the arrivals and departures begin again. . . .

Trains huff clouds of steam, ships hoot cast-off warnings, propellers
revolve, jet engines ignite, women wave to men, men to women
before they climb steps and ramps, turning to wave and look once more

from high decks, top steps, inclined passageways, tinted windows.
Each generation, men and women stitch themselves together,
designing and figuring in their own unique hours-quick or

years-labored tapestry, though no matter how close interwove
the fibers, the cloth always ends in severed threads – but just
before separation by cart, train, boat or plane, before the

scissor blades close, shearing the fabric short, cutting the twain
apart, those moments belong to the woman. Through the years
left her, she will examine the thinning warp and weft of that

last scene, and the many, or few, that came before, devoting
secret hours to repairing the worst moth-nibbled holes and frayed
tears while needle points of memory prick skin, cause blood-red

drops to well and spill, dotting the precious fabric. To this
woman, the constant small stabbing jabs are welcome, reminding
her she still lives, and was once loved –
and for countless other women, in other places,
it is all beginning again.

Castle with Nightingale & Climbing Roses

The Lost Heart – Wayfaring

How Many Miles?

How many miles to Babylon?
    Fourscore and ten.
Can I get there by candlelight?
    Yes, there and back again.
        English Nursery Rhyme

How many miles to your one true love,
    lost from your empty eyes?
The only path is by white starlight,
    curved bright across night skies.
You bide sweet content close beside him
    till steep falls the high dream tide
and you are cast back in bed alone,
    all your tears to be cried.

Three Young Eagles

While you were here they never appeared. You left
and now they have returned, splintering the air
with keening cries that pierce into brain and a

heart filled these late summer days with a lethal
mix of Desire, Anger and Grief that
washes through me from morning rising to

day's end, even infusing bitter poison
into dreams that come with sleep. Hatched this year,
three young eagles with black blotched wings circle

against blue enamel sky, screaming their
unappeasable hunger . . . one eagle for
frustrated Desire . . . one for Anger at

Fate's dictate that prevents resolution –
and toward the person generating this
abrupt drop from decades' concealed cliff onto

unyielding rock . . . one for Grief, that a once-
on-a-time beginning of such Beauty and
Wonder can only remain an aching
Agony of Loss all my days lived this life.

With Time, the young eagles will grow, their cries
diminish, as Time eventually will dull
razor edges of raw feeling, leaving,

finally, of both eagles and emotion,
only a small pile of bones for crows to pick
over, and cinereous ash to scatter

on cool interstellar winds. Today, though,
refusing to stand watching while that Old Ghoul
diminishes the Desire, erases the

Anger and diffuses the Grief, I pound fists
against his moving cart in a vortex of
fury at his dispensation, and try

to stand firm . . . but his juggernaut rolls onward,
inexorable, splintering my bones and
pressing my beating heart's red red blood

into the earth beneath those iron wheels.

Petition

Finally, I'll remember you only as a
near-forgotten fragment of song ghosting bloodless

and faint from fading recollections . . . time was I
could call you instant before me, vivid sum

of persistent, mind-burnt details: tall, tanned frame, spare
hard bones, square shoulders perfect for wearing

uniforms with a careless elegance, close-cropped
hair, prominence of nose, full, sculpted lips, defined

dimpled chin, long-fingered hands with heavy blue
and red rings holding constant cigarettes, voice tone

incisive, words precise, at time bending syntax to complex
games, manner skeptical, brusque with fools, laughter

spontaneous in delight the world's madness, lover's
wit, eyes a piercing blue, cold as arctic glaciers,

then glinting sudden intense tropic warmth. . . .

Today, though, I'll not dwell on these brain-graven
images. The past gone, dead, I swear to no

more haunt your dreams, only petitioning Fates to
let your shade no longer stand by my bedside in

chill, sleepless midnights, and for those Kindly Ones to
blur all pictures of you from sharp-edged memory

so I will be free to slice and bury each piece
of every last negative so far down in

subconscious deeps I may at last know dreamless peace
through all my nights' blackest hours.

A Thin Wind

Often these days I find myself standing on a
high place – bleak boulder-strewn moor or blade sheer cliff rim –

at the dimming edge of twilight whiles a thin wind
from remote distances of the black infinite,

glinting throughout currents of its ceaseless stirring
with trillion millions of darting, spinning star sparks,

lifts my hair, molds and wraps my gown tighter to skin
than winding shroud. No words live in this space suspended

between passion and heartbreak – comes only the
wire-thrumming sound of a knife keen wind slicing

into my limbs with surgical precision.
Excising memory of the next parting from

you, however, will be more difficult than
former amputation, with little chance of

success till mind's overthrow achieved with
        last breath expended.

The Spiral Stair

I missed a step in the dark and came down hard,
bruising my thin skin all over, breaking bones
and my heart. I swear I caught a glimpse of

you on a curve of that stair, in some sort of
ridiculous armor suit medieval –
above or below I hardly know I was

so dizzy with vertigo from the endless
tortuous twists of narrow steepness
spiraling upward and down around the thin

twisting rails of one of those open metal
staircases where you look straight through narrow slats
and see risers both ascend-descend in

diminishing curls. I swear I heard you as
well, clanking in all that metal gear round some
near spiral of that damn stair – forever just

out of sight, receding or preceding me
on the curve ahead or below. My life has
been lived so consistently out of sync with

yours, how the hell should I know? But every
cell of my blood is aware the one way to
find you this fractured millennium will be

 to fling myself over
  the guardian rails,
   gambling the terrifying fall
    into improbability
     is the right direction.

Thief of Dreams

Boy Eros is a larcenous, expert thief,
winging down to steal soft-foot into my room

chill midnights, rob me of the precious jewel
of sleep. When I find I'm being plundered

again, tire of pounding pillows, tucking back
sheets and determine to outwit that wicked child's

scheme – pulling on robe, brewing chamomile tea,
ritually remaking bed before climbing

back in with comforting brew and Shakespeare,
then at last switch off light – it's often only

to find the tormenting lad still there, perched
atop high bookshelf or bedpost finial,

carelessly twirling sleep's sparkling pendant of
dreams, twisting heart-tight its gold chain of longing

till sudden release uncoils it whipping back,
scattering a thousand fractured rainbow

prisms – faceted glimpses I would have
dreamt of you – dancing in tantalizing

splinters across the pale gray wall behind my
eyes, each glittering slice mirroring life-like,

impossible meetings, soft, warm kisses,
cherishing caressings . . . but the bright fragments

spinning so fast elude sense, refusing to
unite in even half-second sequences,

the lost dreams a mirage shimmering beyond
glimmering tears and conscious mind's reach, swiftly

dimming, vanishing in the unfathomed
abyss of broken sleep's departed hours.

October's Forge

Radiant leaves burn away the tissue thin fabric
of brittle October, their falling millions of
heart, oval, palmate, serrate, scimitar and sword shapes

flickering against gray-marbled thunderhead sky as
they spiral in bright descent to lie crisp against wet
cement and shower-slicked grass where, piled in raked heaps,

strewn in hollows and across streets, the varied kinds
faintly glow, rustling in their drying, fading crumble.
These vestiges of coruscating sparks cast from

autumn's luminous forge in arcing sprays of molten
gold, copper, bronze, amber, garnet singe through edges of
my shivering skin, scorch into blood, burn through sinew

and bone to heart muscle and brain tissue where the
candescent embers continue to prick and throb long
after the season when they first caught flame until

the fiery simulacra, consuming themselves,
disintegrate to corpse-gray ashes bleached of passion's
blazing fever and the red sear of memories.

November Rain

The scent of tears: crystallized salt
compound of despair and grief squeezed

from heart's blood in chill pre-dawn hours
when the small brown bird on breastbone

pipes its constant monotonous plaint:
'alone, gone, alone, gone, gone, alone'. . . .

Arrives day's drab light, gray rain burdened clouds
streaking and trickling pale teardrops down the

thin glass membrane dividing bleak outer
world from bleaker within when comes anguished

realization one muck dank November
dark day that these seconds, minutes, hours

of autumn rain are dissolving the precious,
precisely incised cuts of razored pain

in sinew, heart and brain to minutest
grains of mirror-shattered grief, coursing them

through hollow bone spillways inside skin where,
leaching into bloodstream's clamorous red

rush, they whirlpool in needle-tipped atoms
that prick and scrape thread-thin veins raw until

cold Atropos's ice-bright shears slice – and
abruptly beating heart, then racing blood, stops.

Tear-shimmered vision, despising Fate, looks
through streaked panes as season's thousand thousands

frost-seared, wind-dried flame tint leaves decay to
rain-soaked, drab brown and tan, their sodden, shredded

fragments slicking lawns, streets, clogging gutters,
brimming ditches, swirling in water-rush

runnels of pulped and muddy mush till they vanish,
writhing, down gaping sewer gullets straight to Hades.

The Musician

My bones, sinews, veins are become frame and strings
of a harp where your fingers play high octave

clefs to low arpeggios of desire.
As sinews slacken with love and threaten to

wholly unstring me, you tune them to a
higher pitch of unappeasable craving,

your clever hands precisely inscribing
on the parchment of each millimeter of

my skin bass, treble and grace notes, half tones and
semi-quavers in every key imagined,

creating an entire intricate
symphony from the simple but constantly

mode-changing, never repeating melody
and counterpoint of this most ancient of airs.

Fate-set limits of days decree this singing
in the blood cannot last – widening chasms

of distance will separate us, and as years pass
flesh creases and sags and bones turn brittle

while one by one notes and phrases that played
our brief love lyric in blood, muscle and bone

will fade, till finally remains only a
faintest echo from one frayed, soft-plucked string

to vibrate through the three times thousand ice-chill,
star-dusted miles of darkling air between us.

Last Act

In sleep, my heart knows its home, winging faster than
thought to nest in you, whiles for dissolving soap-bubble

seconds in sweet dreams improbable concoctions of
entre-act plots move fast to happy-ever-afters

in the spotlighted sunshine-warm glow before a
dark backdrop curtain. This curtain – dyed deepest black

possible and invariably set behind
the tenderly enacted stage front scenes – hangs from

ropes rigged in the flies, and a lurid, pulsing rim
of red-gold outlines cloth edges and the thin line

along bottom where fabric meets floor. Inch by inch, with
nightmare inevitability, the narrow crack

between boards and curtain hem increases, the red glare
flaring to baleful burning sulphur in widening

gap until – abrupt and startling always – the drop
curtain jerks, billows briefly outward, then lifting straight

up, disappears. And I'm inside a different story
with a last act script that ends the same way every time:

a woman standing alone on an empty stage, bucket
and brush nearby, the flat drained light of a rainy

autumn day leaking through a few high, grimed windows.
Though she's wearing the rags for a Cinderella part,

there's certainly no fairy godmother in sight, and
the woman is clutching the long handle on a mop

of wrung-out, wet and dirty rope strands for dear life.

To the Kindly Ones

From a haze-pale afternoon sky, grace can
befall in the span of a sparrow's wing beat.

You – the one destined, desired from world's end
to world's end – there, on a mundane corner
sidewalk at the crossing of two streets, waiting.

Three times lost, most dearly won of my life's loves,
may the Kindly Ones permit – at the halt of

some rough track twisting steep upward till stopped
abrupt at high piled boulders blocking sight
of the country beyond – that I, impelled by

causeless hope and regardless of bruised skin,
torn fingers, bleeding feet may climb on, crossing

over the barrier peaks' stony gray spines to
see unfurl beyond a rainbow tapestry
threaded here-there with glints of silver-gilt:

firs and pines slope to flowering meadows where
crystal streams run into sparkling sapphire

lakes, patchwork hills – fruiting orchards, emerald
pastures, tilled fields, hedgerows, copses, tidy farms –
bow up and down, turreted castles perch on

beetling crags above bends of a wide river
flowing through valley dotted with plaster and

wood villages . . . in a fold of those pastel
hills I will at last walk down a familiar
poplar bordered road ending in an arch

of time-worn stone and enter a manor
courtyard – corner towers, peaked gables, diamond

pane lattice windows, cerise and gold roses
clambering sun warmed walls – to find you there,
waiting once more, in the heart of my heart's home.

Confetti Snow

I hold you in my thoughts through my days' hours as
the central figure standing in a crystal globe.

When I tilt this glass-clear mind bubble slightest
degree, thousands of weightless white confetti

snowflakes swirl up – swarming, surrounding then falling
slowly back over your paint-bright, frozen form,

piling thick-layered white on your head, shoulders and
around your legs. I think of white down filling white

quilts and white pillows while I lie on white sheets
listening to your even, quiet breathing and

steady heartbeats until you rouse and we begin
once more that sweet immemorial strife of need to
join two separates into one being, briefly complete.

When I die, slice through my veins with sharpest knife
and no red blood will flow – only a slow seep of

weightless confetti snow crystals will come trickling
to pool around my corpse till a small rising wind

whirls the fast-melting-to-transparence ice atoms
    into infinity's fathomless aetherial oceans
flowing through eternity's forever expanding skies.

Summer Day

Your longer stride measured to mine, we walk beside each other,
shadows joined, along a country lane in distant sun-drenched clime,

talking of important insignificant things beneath high
overarching canopy of honey-locust trees. Slightest warm

air current stirs the countless stems, and the myriad pinnate leaves
tremble and twist, sere surfaces chafing, while this rustling pierced

roof – constantly revealing-concealing heat-bleached sky behind –
delicately flicks us with its million weightless shade-tongues as we

move through the trunks' mottled colonnade supporting the simmering
weight of atmosphere with its thick suspension of scent atoms:

dust, peat, rock, dry grass, moss. At some remark of mine, near place track
begins curving in a wide bend, you turn to me, slow smile etching
      creases around your glinting blue eyes. Here you stop –

but my steps continue, inexorably pulled along the path's
slowly increasing arc, leading me to abrupt plunge over

concealed knife-edge cliff and into long flailing fall through decades of
heartbreak exile in a chill north zone of overcast skies, spiked

firs, ice-defined mountains. There, daily sight of those peaks' glacier-honed,
razor-edge shapes slice into mind's eye, cutting repeatedly from

brain to skin to bone, creating over years an intricate mesh
of blood-seeping nerve ends patterning my flesh. Now, in my later

age, slightest touch anywhere from neck to groin to ankle and all
points between instantly begins chain reaction of twinge and sting

on a body become strange tally marker: each incised cut preserves
score of every hour apart from you and precise record of
      every distant, bitter mile from your heart.

The Whetted Blade

Remembrance hones its bright bladed knife
on memory's whetstone most potently
in the black blind watches of night, its
steel blade polishing to a silvered

mirror reflecting images and sounds
that slice shaking soul to minced splinters:
tone of your voice, timbre of laughter,
glance from those blue eyes glinting with a

growing smile, expressive trick of your
eyebrows, sudden tenderness or swift
roughness of urgent intimate need,
a turn of your head, the feel of your hands . . .

though I close eyes against such lightning shafts
glancing off grief's bleak edge, in darkness
the tears well, overspilling eyes in
brine-stinging streams, seeping slow salt-crust tracks

down my cheeks – till one sleep-eluding, black
chasmed midnight I at last grasp that sharp
sheening blade and drive its fine wicked point
straight into my persistent beating heart . . .

as warm, vein-red blood pools about my corpse,
tranquil sleep will descend, weightless, silent –
in snow-white cloud-quilt of feathers plucked by
merciful angels from their stainless wings.

Heartbreak

Funny about a heart's breaking –
I thought it would happen once with

a tearing, ripping kind of hollow
crunch, and afterward, for years, one

would be left sweeping knife-slicing
shards and needle-stabbing splinters

with broom into pan – left-over
detritus of that inconvenient

throbbing organ which then, mortally
wounded, would soon prove – one hoped –

a hollow shell and quite utterly *dead*.

Instead I find, dismayed, the traitor
heart, phoenix-like, rebirths itself

after every crisis of longing
and grief, creating itself whole

once more in a burst of gut-igniting,
entrail-burning orange bitter flame

that it might, at some *useless* random
memory's prick, fracture afresh –

jagged fragments flying everywhere,
sharp pieces needing to be swept up,

tossed in dust-bin all over again.

Chrysalis

Spirit spins a chrysalis from longing and grief,
hatching a pale butterfly beating frail wings against
Fate's implacable black granite walls – walls that rise

higher with each inch gained of straining flight till at
last the creature falls back, spent, before venturing
opposite direction across bone-bleached desert

where no leaf or grass blade grows, the only sound the
keening of a relentless Boreal wind that soon
shreds the insect's wings into broken, open webs.

Exhausted, it drops and crawls about the sand, but finding
no drop of moisture in the burning emptiness
expires, leaving only small husk soon crumbled by

restless Zephyrs' transparent fingers to soft dust,
the minuscule grains blowing through their careless hands,
swift-scattering to farthest reaches of universe.

Caprice of the Gods in some far off millennium
may permit diademed Clotho gather together

such insignificant atoms again, and star-robed
Lachesis spin them into plot diverging from this

of parting and tears. Divine Whim *may* rule kindlier
tale, but the Eldest Sister wielding silver-bright shears

ensures the invariable ending of sharp loss and
bitter grief allotted mortals from time's beginning.

      Petition Them for what you will –
         forget Her at your Peril.

The Orchard Meadow

Odd times those few days I would see a certain
reckless gaiety of word and act I understood

not usual to you – engendered, perhaps, by complete
displacement from normal routine, though I suspect

caused more by understanding you have moved through
a life rich and long beyond expectation

only to arrive, astonished to some degree, at
this new place with another being – hardly known

though familiar as your own blood – yet, as your habit,
accepting the Dispensation that drew us here

as you have accepted all the provisions of
The Kindly Ones – not as your due, but rather with

a quick, full appreciation that has accrued
into the vibrant brightness surrounding one

enjoying, for some star-writ reason, the favor
of The Three Fates who, women that they are, were

possibly susceptible as I to the smile that
only grew more devastating as you matured.

So cause enough for laughter, and even for your
occasional carelessness in throwing away –

if only for minutes – of watchful stance and that
deliberation of manner so intrinsic

to your being. With Their Aid, after all, you
outfoxed Mortality often enough – what

reason then for you not to delight in an
unexpected sunset stroll through an orchard

meadow where you are licensed to freely pluck up
and sample the unexpected windfall of sweet

ripe fruit spread there for your private delectation?

The tears in this do not pertain to you. I
gather them in vessels of chaste silver to place

at Their Perfect Feet, requisite Thank Offering
for the hours that so swiftly splintered into

knife point shards of seconds stabbing my heart with each
drawn breath through the few days allotted me with you.

The Raveled Shift

Golden threads of longing, silver threads of grief
streak the fabric of my life. Daylight's swift dropping

shuttle of rayed hours looms and infills over-
under the shining silver and gold fillet strips,

concealing them beneath a complex tissue of
thoughts, acts, syntax. Comes black night, the twists and tendrils

of day's cloth unstring back to open webbing of
thinnest metal-glinting filaments. Clad in

this flimsy spider-gauze I wander dark vaulted
tunnels, tight-slit windowless corridors, climb

up, down Piranesian stairs cut off mid-air,
and confront at every level and turn closed doors –

iron bolts, hasps, hinges, straps, studs, fierce locks – always
seeking one rimmed in hair's-breadth of gold I know will

open into a fire-lit room: bay windows
diamond paned, some inset with stained glass medallion

shields or painted Gothic-lettered Latin mottoes,
book-lined walls, carpet of a thousand twining

Persian flowers before carved, columned fireplace
and mantel where, ensconced in high-back brocaded

armchair, you sit, reading. At sudden, slight draft you
glance up, then after marking place you close book, and

    your blue eyes looking direct at me, you smile.

One night, I stumble on a door outlined in a
pulsing gold dazzle, without knob or latch. It

resists push, but I pound and pound, breaking nails,
running splinters in fingers, bruising wrists till at

last it grudges open – but instant my foot
crosses threshold every gold spark extinguishes –

and I am sitting up in my narrow bed, clutching
my own bone-sharp elbows, shivering, not one

raveled thread of shift left to clothe flesh exposed
    entirely naked in blade cold night air.

They Loved Me They Said

They loved me, they said to the child, but they
took her away from the person loved above

all others in the child's world. You loved me,
you said once to the woman, but then you

went away, disappearing as you had twice
before. One plus two plus the early one makes

four times the fall down sheered-off knife cliffs of loss
with the slow climb back to a life never the

same the other side that deep, steep rock canyon
of grief and the river running salt tears there.

What is left after these unmoorings of
self from the beloved? After useless nights

weeping, often arrives soul-wrenching anger,
head and stomach stabbing pain, then years to

manage best as one may with life left, while
hoping somewhere deep in subconscious fragile

seedling of perspective might sprout, and with time's
passing grow into plant bearing tentative,

pale leaves of resignation. Friends offer
distraction to certain degree, and delving deep

in art and music studies; but above all
creation of worlds where soul-self escapes along

new pathways into distant landscapes provide
refuge and reason to go on – and even

faintest hope one of these tracks may wend, some
unimaginable day, unto heart's lost

home. It cannot surprise, though, at end of this
fate-allotted span, if tears blur tired eyes when

looking through all those years' drawings of never
realized, happy-ever-after dreamlands,

and spirit plunges once more into that profound
hope-lost abyss shaded yet blacker ebon

with approaching demise. Might I discover
then – if the gods of their grace and power

decree – at that last light-flickering into purest
    carbon-black moment the stars glitter
        brightest in darkest night?

The Small Dun Bird

Beyond steep, wild white waterfalls of separation
lie cobalt-black, fathoms drowned-deep oceans of grief,
and storm-shattered wreck on pitch black nights' knife-fanged reefs.

After, in a winter bleak landscape of leaf-stripped
trees, arrives a small dun bird to sit on breastbone's
skeleton branch, where it flutters weakly, piping in

monotonous, wearying voice though every hard-won day's
hour to remind of the blade in my heart – that last
sight of you, walking away, into memory's cold,

cloud-obscured shadow land. I cling to your brief pause to
look back at me as drowning woman to thrown life raft.

> Somewhere,
> beyond ice-bitter winter, lies another country.

In a brick walled garden, summer's amber luster sheens
a glossy iridescence on petals of citron
roses, lilies, jessamine, clove gillyflowers,

pulsing spiced scents within the slight moving shimmers of
warm air. Slowly the golden hours burn to drowsed noontide.
A green dragonfly, glass-transparent wings vibrating,

hovers at trickling fountain basin, and small birds
flutter among tall dill plants gone to seed by cascades of
twining woodbine. The gate latch clicks – a metallic snick

sharp in the warm air. You are there, motionless for
suspended moment, head aureoled those split seconds
by flashing, yellow-gilt feathers of goldfinches put

to startled flight – and when you begin walking toward
me I see you moving through a dazzlement of bright
wings shattering, scattering the sun-sparked, prismed light.

Litter

This shiny plastic up-to-the-nanosecond
world we've constructed: cell phones, emails, texting,

'partners', 'significant others', guilt-absolving
analysis, and pills, pills, pills – has small provision

for the delirious extremes of passion – untidy,
inconvenient emotion that now seems oddly

old-fashioned, thriving better by far in atmosphere
replete with feathered hats, Hussar uniforms, tight-laced

corsets, lace-up boots, lace-edged petticoats, sheets and
pillowcases, Fabergé trifles, giddy Strauss waltzes,

cursive penmanship, cut crystal ink standishes,
echoing glass-roofed stations and steam-puffing trains.

Still, even in the present diminished mundane, as
you walk along – say choosing for convenience smooth path

beside rail track – unexpected vibration of ground
beneath your feet can occur. Surprised, you look around

and see on track far behind faint light of an engine
approaching round a curve you never noticed. For a

moment you glance away – time aplenty to move to
safety – but with lightning speed the train arrives and

                Bam!
you're blown sideways and fall flat on face, overwhelmed.

The train screams away, rapidly distance diminished to
toy's insignificance. If you are among the fortunate –

tossed wide, not mangled to bleeding pulp – eventually
you stagger upright again, though for the miles of your

life's journey remaining, you discover gouged-out bits
of bloodied skin and white needle-splintered bone shards –

    all recognizably once yours – strewn unsightly
        about, littering path and grassy verges.

The Iron-Locked Coffer

As miser does with precious hoard, at night I lift
treasured images of you from iron-banded,
triple-locked coffer where they stay safe hid in daylit

hours. Even without candles to lumine obscure
midnight, each likeness pulses with so strong an inner
light it shines clear, allowing my every feeling nerve

to pass over your features, your hands and limbs, your stance,
your very manner of being again and again.
Once I feared this oft-repeated butterfly brush

of soul against these portraits and their recurring
exposure in remembrance's spotlight would, with time's
elapse, blur them, but as years pass I find, unlike

photographs passing decades fade, these pictures formed of
elements far stronger than ink on paper stay
detail bright, burning with a surreal inward glow

imparted in their forging on the scorching, white-hot
anvil of desire. These images are there wrought as
shapes on coins from a platinum so pure no slightest

adulteration of baser metal dims their silver-white
luster, then each one placed – with longing's repeated
hammer-beat – inside heart's most secret chamber, and there

engraved with memory's stabbing needle-point tools to
high, precise relief. After separation's fiery
tempering, the coin-portraits plunged in cold northern sea

of salt tears where the icy brine instantly seals the
new-graved delineations in hard carapace of
frozen mind-ice – thus, however oft examined, the

coined icons never lose brilliance or crisp outline.
A certain danger manifests over time, though, in
rims of these glittering circles. Years of repeated

handling wear outer margins to a honed knife edge
until a network of cuts crisscrosses my fingers
and palms from countless nights turning each medallion's

picture this way, that to study from every angle.
Easy now to take one silver-sheened razor-blade round
and with decisive motion slice its keen verge across

wrists' thin skin, continuing incision straight down through
tendon gristle, and watch, mesmerized, as the gaudy,
warm drench slicks, then melts the chill, vitrified surfaces

of the lap-piled iced-silver coin effigies that gleamed
silver-gilt deceit through too many dark nights . . . the
sticky red rush first washes the platinum blood-scarlet,

then transforms ever darker garnet till finally
only corroded metal particles dissolving
into carbonized black ashes are left to drift,
      settle on a pale still corpse.

Beyond the Black Curtain

Isn't lost love the truest love since all love is lost
at that end where, surprised by years, one arrives

diminished and much nearer being's essence – thinned hair, thin
blood, skin, sinew, bone and – if fortunate in genes –

a few bundles of brain synapse electrodes still
connected, more or less, transmitting rational sense.

Standing there, I'll turn briefly to glance back on the
fleeting moments of life's delight: sun slants that

ignite autumn foliage to transparent flame,
precise-sliced amethyst and cobalt facets of

horizon mountains against rain-rinsed spring sky,
a hummingbird's vibrating wings suspending the

prism-feathered cerise-green-black atomy in
air, and last – what else but the slow heartbreak smile

of a long-lost, three-thousand miles distant lover?
A sigh for the heartache this smile brought – so many

useless salt tears, sleepless nights – then, too weary to
go on as corporeal form, my shade will walk forward

    into descending velvet folds of absolute dark.

If that enveloping black curtain ever lifts,
sudden light will strike so nuclear white on sight

accustomed to black naught it can only transform
spirit vision utterly . . . through revelation's

burning haze, a luminous pathway may emerge. . . .
With cautious, tentative paces, I will begin

journeying up, over, round and through hills, dales,
rivers, plains, until one day soul-self's eyes discern –

distant-small, but lucid as illumination
in book of hours – buff, dusty track leading

into dense wood then switching up steep slope past firs
to emerald meadow on mountain's gray shoulder,

diamond flashing stream, sapphire lake close by
near hut on rock ledge, ghost chimney smoke wavering

into azure air. I hasten toward this path to
heart's inmost hope, but stumble over hidden rocks,

fall into muck-brown swamp – slimy weeds entangle limbs
and gnats sting – flailing, floundering, I achieve

mud-slick verge of foot-sucking gunk, and step by
labored step clamber up long incline to scrubby waste

where barberry, gorse and thorn reach raking claws, wandering
unmarked hours there till stopped by thick hedge of twisted

briars wove with spiked firethorn. On and on I trudge
beside, but find no exit gate or path – then understand

sole way out is to push in, thrash passage through regardless
of spiders, spiny gashes and back-whipped branches.

Emerging at last, bitten, slashed, stung, garments in shreds,
again I glimpse, on alp above another stand of firs,

the wildflower sprinkled meadow, brook, lake and chalet.
Without backward glance, I plunge beneath tall, frowning trees.

Boughs lash and snap, roots trip, brambles, nettles scratch as I
struggle in matted, snarled undergrowth through closing

day's dim light and into a waning moon's spectral night.
Moths beat pale wings up and down slanting moon rays and great

beasts breathe and pant at my back while eyes high and low in
every glade glow with eerie phosphor incandescence.

As pearl-white dawn filters between trunks, I finally
emerge from trees to see track clear before me and speed

uphill through meadow and around lake to mount log stair
and arrive heart-skipping breathless on chalet's top step.

Seconds suspend to an eternity longer than
years' wanderings . . . but before my raised hand knocks, you

open the door and I enter in my heart's home – that
dwelling place constantly sought and so stubbornly

held to through the slow clock-tock hours of starless nights'
fears and the sun-wind-rain of life's ever-receding

weeks-months-years. It matters not the Fates grant five
    minutes-hours-days or *decades* with you – it will
        never be enough.

The Golden Key

Decades after, Fate's caprice allows unlooked-for
benison – you return me the golden key I thought
forever lost. I lower the lid on Grandmother's

rosewood desk, my eyes moving from row of cubby
holes down to three narrow drawers above blotter, the
lowest outlined with hair's breadth of light and where I

see white incandescence begin to flare and pulse through
the miniature brass-edged keyhole. Hand weighing the
little key, I pause, fearful of opening after

so many years – and think of panicked nights dream-prisoned
in lightless rooms, blind, breathless in smother-thick velvet
black and falling, crawling, groping every inch of a

splintered floor, seeking the key that will unlock door and
open into day's dazzling sunshine. I turn the key,
pull drawer, reach to sort small stash of framed photographs

jumbled within, and discover gilt paint chipped, wood cracked,
covering glass fractured. As I lift and examine
each one, razor-edge shards spill over my hands, slicing

fine red lines from finger-tips to wrists, some piercing to
bone, while tiny, angle-spiked sun prisms glance off the
blade keen barbs, stabbing upward and pricking eyes to

sudden vision-blurring tears. Blinking, impatient, I
brush away the prickling salt liquid, arrange pictures
in correct sequence of years, and begin to

perceive my life's recurring pattern – people, places
that mattered most always gone away, disappeared,
removed from hearing, touch and sight of child and woman

    both – my enduring days into years legacy,
      this one of distance, loss and tears.

It is far too late, now, to return you the key, even
if I could summon the strength. I will clasp it secure
around my neck on platinum chain, and have it always

by my heart. Then, at the end, the key is near to use
once more . . . softly, the polished rosewood drawer will glide
open, revealing those precious, soul-seared images

from the lost long ago concealed within – and your
figure, still luminescent, gold-aureoled, infused
with the silver-deliberate cadences of your voice –

that I may take bright remembrance of these with me,
                into the star-streaked dark.

Falling Star

How should I my true love know,
from others come a-courting?

By his smile and eyes sky blue,
and fine gilt-corded silver shoon.

He fell from a star into my life
one sun-struck noontide in spring:

around him golden arrows rained –
flaming points straight-aimed darts to

an unprotected heart. Desire,
ignited, seared scars that pulse still,

with never cure found late or soon –
not standing stripped in arctic sleet,

glacial mountain lakes, nor the ice-frost
chill of a waning winter moon.

Two Minute Film Clip
'Woman Looking Out Window'

A cool spring evening – last embers of dusk fading in clear
northwest sky. Furred apricot haloes surround streetlamp globes

just flickering on, their light reflecting on gray pavement.
In a second-story bay window, a young woman

stands watching – in moments, from apartment entrance below,
a tall man exits and crosses street to car, stepping

into a circle of brightness that illumines the
olive-drab uniform, gilds his brown hair, shows up his

characteristic quick yet deliberate movements. He
unlocks trunk, lifts in cloth suitcase, closes lid with

hollow thunk, then opens driver's door – it shuts with crisp
metallic snap. The engine starts and the woman watches

as the car moves down the quiet street and out of sight.

Four decades later I am still the woman in the window,
this film strip unspooling in my mind for the thousandth

time: you cross a street into a spotlight of apricot
radiance that dusts you with atoms of pulsing gold, then

you drive slowly away. I think you glance up once as the
car rolls off – and I am left standing in a dusk-filled room.

Need deeper than love, molten in muscle and blood – a spark
flying from Vulcan's anvil as the celestial smith

hammered a new star arced through the welkin and scorched both
our souls. But sundering tides of circumstance forever

pull us apart to an unnatural separation that
aches in spaces between sinews and bones, pricks in each

blood cell every day's minute and year's hour until
my ending when spirit, unmoored from mortal flesh, will

float into air, fleeting arrow-swift to you. If you are
vanished from place sought, soul-self – wound about in shadow

shroud, desolate beyond tears – is Fate-destined to endlessly
wander firmament's starry trails and shimmering black

infinities, forever seeking you, my lost heart's lost home.

Nuclear Winter

In love of a certain magnitude – if you survive
that initial blast to reel staggering away from

black fallout cloud – it's guaranteed one day while still
negotiating the strewn ruins of your life some

fragment of sharp shattered mirror will reveal eyebrows
entirely singed off, eyes' pupils dilated to wide

shocked stare. As you lurch and totter along wearing
your expression of ambushed surprise, attempting

to distance self from the catastrophe behind, you
realize, from glances cast your way by passersby,

something else amiss – looking down, you find every
covering garment blown off or shredded, the rags yet

there more oval holes than clothes that decently conceal
your bruised skin from intrusive gazes. You stumble on,

trying to maintain straight line though constantly missing the
pathway and finding yourself scrambling up high stony

passes, pushing through dense forests, wobbling across dry
wastes strewn with barbed shrubs. From head to feet, you are slashed

by jagged rocks, jabbed by twigs, stabbed by thorns till the last
cloth fragment disintegrates and you are stripped bare

beneath an indifferent heaven's blue dome. On you
blunder, thirsting, flesh alternately goose-bumped or

fever-baked, when, at slight dip in the ground, you come on
a heaped gray fur cape. Gathering this plush weight round your

nakedness, you move slowly forward, to discover
only frozen barrens stretching every direction – a

desolation of white, wind-scoured ice stretching farther
      than spirit can bear to chart or map.

Soul's Vessel

Buried deep in my skin, in some half millimeter
space between tiniest of interlocking bones,
or in some disregarded pinpoint interstice

of convoluted cranium, there must linger
faintest trace of how I was before the fact of your
existence invaded every corner of my body's

being – from beating heart to toes and up to eyes and
sentient mind, filling every least pore and smallest
capillary between, tingling every atom I

own with awareness of your changing expressions,
the taste of your skin, the hard feel of your bones – and
waking instantly the ancient imperative that

sings and surges in racing blood, throbs in every blue
vein, swells soft tissues in breasts, belly and groin and
makes my existence's only wish to fall flat, open

legs wide for you to plunge inside, driving deeper and
deeper till all consciousness extinguished of the
woman previous. But once past those wildest moments

of conjunction – when even memory that
earlier woman despised – miniscule iota
of first self still flickers, persistent, in response to

uneasy premonition . . . a realization this
prior being cannot be erased entire – she
may provide only vessel that will carry my past

and present selves to another, gentler country on the
rising, inexorable tide of salt tears soon to
draw this new, erotically bewitched self into a

fathoms-deep desolation of 'afterward' beyond
all known landmarks and extending into a surging
ocean waste of separation, its fierce currents

carrying my frail barque farther away each day from
the one blood-clamored, heart-desired beloved.

Chain of Fire

In the lost long ago, a day sparked in sun fire
combined unstable elements – blood red kinship and
white hot desire – into a golden chain joining

two into one . . . for a time-warped span of noon to
twilight hours, molten heat from the new-forged links seared
through the woman's skin, imprinting a blazon on her

trembling heart. But the delicate, new-forged links prove
fragile, the fine chain snapping with distance, thin metal
dissolving in corrosive salt tears, and the woman for

thrice tens of years, desolate, soul-displaced, wanders from
scorching desert wastes to ice-encased wilderlands. Step
by wrong-footed step, over decades, she treads a

snarled course while mind constructs cage of close-set steel bars
around her burned and fractured heart to forestall slightest
chance of another such disintegration. Until

abhorred Atropos lifts shears one night – a death occurs
and tiny hole snipped in welkin; Clotho spins new thread
on her distaff, and Lachesis weaves it into the

fabric of two severed lives . . . sweet Aphrodite,
rose-fragranced breath, opal-feathered doves on white shoulders,
stands forth against Nyx's night hung backcloth that, shaken

slightly by Eros, the love goddess's constant
attendant, sifts glimmer-gold star motes around her
flawless form that float to earth below. One white arm lifts,

her hand gestures, graceful – and two people meet once more,
the metal bars about the woman's heart melting in
a flare of lightning-shattered seconds. Instantly, a

new chain forged – this of tempered, tensile steel – and the
woman finds, surprised, love strangely renewed in the
falling tide of life's days. A grass plot, daisy starred,

bounded by high, precise hedges becomes hers to
cultivate and protect – a small enclosure where, at
times, another enters in. And once, twice, pulled by that

burnished, remade chain, she flees south a short span of days,
though when returned to the clouded north, some few black nights –
while less often than in years before – she still starts awake,

    choking on salt bitter grief welling from soul's darkest
        depths at iron-hard facts of circumstance.

Gold Suns, Sapphire Oceans

A warm, sun-struck afternoon in the blue long ago,
a uniformed man in high wing-back chair, speaking . . .

in deeps of celestial space, one molten spark of
millions cast from Vulcan's heat-crimsoned anvil arcs

away, travels through time-warped epochal distances
in split seconds to strike, shiver, shatter into an

aureole of spiked gold around the man's head, while
arrows tipped with garnet-glowing fire pierce skin and

lance into heart and soul of woman sitting across,
marking her for life. A few hours after, with

magic's abruptness, a scrim of indigo aether
waterfalls around these two – commotion and sound,

confused colors and shapes vanishing as they begin
a brief duet, spotlighted in the white, fever-bright

blaze of desire. In the spangled air of a
dazzling new country, the woman, flinging soul from self,

executes vaulting leaps, high extensions, whip turns
with flawless star ballerina ease, every move

anticipated, supported as her partner
catches, carries, spins, lifts her in their mad pas de deux.

No happy ending to this tale, though, just stale old
scenario: man leaves, woman left desolate to

discover, as landscape of her life reappears, that
with his departure one-time familiar world grown

alien. Bereft, she first waits, suspended, then
searches, but rushing air currents pile ever higher,

thicker cloud-cumulus ramparts between. She tries
fitting others in that heart space he occupied,

but none return lost sense of joy and completion to
soul's core – at last, disheartened, she buries memories,

builds another life as decades pass, but heart wounds
sustained that blue afternoon never heal. Throbbing at

slightest touch, they persistently seep minute red beads
that trace fine stain lines on milk-pale breasts, and in darkest

nights of grayest days, and certain sun-drenched afternoons,
the woman resolves, at her end, to pray the gods to strike
    her with their red-gold sun arrows once more.

Shadeless nuclear incandescence will dissolve flesh
and bone, ignite a Catherine wheel of flame spinning

glittering fire-filaments into a twisted
cord of luminescence suspended over roaring

abysses of blue-black aeons and sky-high, fathomless
sapphire oceans washing among gold suns, orbiting

planets and pivoting constellations of a
countless billion burning, gyring, swirling galaxies.

For hollow eternities, past all reason, the
woman follows the luminous, thin-stretched causeway. . . .

A capricious god relenting, one particular
millennial moment in farthest space she arrives

a crossing place where long-slant sword shafts of pulsing
light silently clash – here, in this numinous golden

haze, the form of a tall man, eyes glinting summer blue,
emerges – and at last she is gathered in arms that

    create the only home her sharp-pierced, weary
        heart ever desired.

Heart's Home

Love is simple, with presence: timbre and
cadence of a voice in a room, a glance or
handclasp, a smile, a reaching out in the dark.

Love becomes complex, with separation.
Every mile apart equals that much more
pain from increased space between – multiply

this by thousands and the total sum amounts
to more than body and grieving brain can bear.
Either the strain starts fragmenting self into

so many crazed shards both love and lover
have to be exorcised, or self in its
thin skin must begin inhabiting a

different house than before: one life on top floor,
another in basement beneath in soul's deep core
where lies heart's hidden, rediscovered home.

Over time, practice makes moving between these
levels easier, though without doubt it's
an uncomfortable way to live – even dangerous.

Disorientation can strike in an instant's
forgetfulness – were you going up or down
that sharp angled twist of stair? You turn, then

turn about again, confused, miss a step
and take a nasty spill, banging against
sharp edges, acquiring empurpling bruises,

run-in splinters and a bleeding gash to add
to your collection of scrapes, cuts and swollen
lumps. I'd not recommend living this way –

certainly it's not to be tried unless
circumstances and distances desperate.
Choice? A luxury never offered me . . .

once-in-a-life love can hit you like that.

Terminal

There's something to be said, I suppose, for getting through
what you know will prove likely the worst moments of your life

relatively early – or any rate previous the
harm or death one day inevitable for those dear to

you, or advent of seconds designated for your own
    always hoped-not but odds-on painful demise.

Such mundane moments, too – just a tall, lean man, white-haired,
walking away in the fluorescent glare of a cavernous,

over-bright airport terminal . . . you hand in ticket, have
luggage and self scanned, step onto moving stairs, walk through

shadeless halls, then sit, wait on a plastic chair – this limbo
is where the seep of salt tears begins that will continue

for years – then at amplified announcement, another queue
and you're swallowed inside a vermiform tube that ejects

you within an airplane's rumbling insides . . . other people
of course are everywhere – around, before, behind, in lounge

and lines, close following onto crowded plane: mothers with
restless children, teen-agers in jeans, briefcase carrying

types in business dress, young, middle-aged and graying package
vacationers returning from the sunny south. Somehow,

though, none of them quite present to you – not in echoing
corridors or even crammed on plane, for you are become

a stiff-jointed manikin, jerking through prescribed repertoire,
and surrounding chaos doesn't so much as scratch your

shellacked wood shell. Finally, in a fit of vibration, whine
and push-back pressure, the plane lifts off – but you're certainly

no longer entirely there. How could you be, with heart left
behind, pulsing blood all over a polished lino floor,

and soul flown from you, suspended somewhere between earth and
air, but abruptly discovered not lodged any more in what

had seemed, before, its own secure home in a well-guarded
       part of cranium's tight-crammed gray matter.

After this, even when your ultimate end arrives, it
should hold little anguish or even surprise, but provide

more a sense of relief – at last you can stop trying
to fill out a skin and bone garment that no longer

       fits your size –
   and hasn't, for quite some time.

The Way Home

Even after all these years, there's still no sense
or logic in it – a man's voice and laugh, and

a gray day turns to sunshine . . . later, at night,
useless salt tears often come seeping. Just a

man, no schoolgirl dream – once a soldier, then
teacher-scholar, plays tennis, now older, lean

and tanned, round-shouldered, ears stick out a bit,
perhaps too much Roman nose in his ageing

face – wife died, three children plus grandkids, two cats,
and now the problems that come with years. But O!

Those blue blue eyes and intent straight gaze that sees
so deep in me – it compasses my soul, piercing
to my inmost core of being.

I will take the memory of your smile with me,
into the dark, and it will light my way home –
an arrow's arc through the stars direct to your heart.

At the Fleeting Edge of Dreams

On the fugitive edges of my dreams, you are
always going from me, leaving for days, months, years:
you tread down spiral stairs away from tapestry hung,

canopied bed in tower room – descend to oak grove
and tethered horse from daisy-spangled grass slope beneath
massive stone rampart where heaven-high lark song fell

around us as we loved – you ride away on switchback
track from rocky spur where crimson pennons flutter from a
castle's capped turrets and disappear round curve leading

into a dense forest's dusky shade. Once I caught glimpse
of you leaving me where I lay on grass thick with
bluebells in a birch grove, a nearby river's rush

masking sound of your horse trotting off; another time
below a hard cobalt sky you stride from me down a
pillared colonnade, a white-gold sun striking sparks off

ochre walls and orange tile roofs while a hot wind blew
pink almond blossoms through the air, strewing torn petals
along the paving of the sun-slashed, shade-striped walk.

Every time you leave, returning to your other lives,
I wish a chill little draft blow sometimes through a small
hole arrow-shot by Aphrodite's winged attendant

into your breastbone straight to your heart. I should not feel
so alone in my longing then, as I move through hours,
days, years of my life loving others, working – and

always waiting: until that moment I again find
myself standing in certain anticipation at
the top of curling tower stairs – on the cliff beneath

gray castle on headland above a restless sea where
breakers crash over black rocks – beside gate of crag-perched
keep in jag-toothed mountain range – under twinkling spring

leaves in glade by a river – or standing in light and
shade-dappled arcade watching fountain centered in Moresque
tiles toss water diamonds into heat-shimmered air.

One day at our present lives ending, if a god smiles,
it may be we will find each other beneath the light of
farther stars, and perchance the silver-gilt rays falling

there will scribe on meadow grass, leaves, rock and running stream
a different tale, and their kindlier light guide us to place
we may dwell together for spacious span of seasons

that will forever fleet too swiftly by. Now, I step
forth toward my apportioned days' end, Fate-destined to
wait for you again – my soul twin who holds always the

part of my heart that fled my breast when first we met,
      and you looked at me, and smiled.

Shadows under the Pines

A man and a woman walk arm in arm on
dusty track beneath high-arced, twisted pines

in strong noon sunlight, their two shadows close-joined,
delicate tracings of gray lace needle shades

ghosting over them. They pause, become entwined,
one dark joined shadow stretching long behind.

Cicadas' rasp-scratch from every tree branch and
faintest air breaths flow around warm rocks, drawing

pungent scent from scrub rosemary and thyme –
far below, scatterings of gilt-brilliant coins

coruscate on a silk-sheened, azure sea.

When I move apart from you and begin to
walk away, my shadow separates from yours,

extending, thinning with each farther step
until, looking round, I find you lost from view,

and my own soul-shadow going from me.
I stand, heart-sight watching, heart-sick within, as

the near-transparent woman-shade vanishes,
fleeing back to join with you and pass into

that other life Fate never permitted me.

Orphan Phantoms, Reaching

All the words I never spoke, all the embracings,
twinings, couplings never realized, the journeys,
conversations, meals, laughter and tears never shared

between us – these shades of days, months, years of a life
never achieved I bequeath to you, my spirit twin
and heart's home. Departing my present envelope

of skin, blood and bone, I will cast from me every
last pallid ghost – wan attendants of my soul through
long decades – that they may haunt you to your end and

even after, in those starry fields where souls wander
beyond this life. These wraiths will not come as banshees
frighting you awake by their wailing and rending of

garments, nor chain-clanking specters pronouncing ghastly
dooms to make you start awake, eyes wide, hair on end. . . .
No, my projected phantoms will reveal themselves starved,

diaphanous orphan waifs, pearl pellucid tears
falling from huge eyes, streaking pale countenances as
they reach transparent hands to gently tug edges of

your sleeping spirit to make you stir and turn, then smile
as you dream of Paradise meadows where you stroll with
the one lover desired above all others, and

lie with her on feathered grasses amongst blue speedwell
and forget-me-nots close by tinkling crystal stream whilst
wandering zephyrs – wings fanning sweet perfumes through

azure air, invisible fingers caressing your
skin – whisper of a glimmering realm hid behind
disappeared years of once-upon-a-time in the

cloud-shadowed land of might-have-been. Perchance, though, one
moping sprite's sigh may remind of a certain past hour's
surprised delight – bright chance that offered you unknown

country to explore, even inhabit – had you not
turned from me and walked briskly away in the apricot
twilight of a cool spring evening, your tall figure dissolving,

>   then vanishing into the remote, immeasurable
>   distances of the lost long ago.

Sun Blindness

A sun-bright spring day – a breezy short trip on
painted white-green ferry, sunlight scattering

molten, glitter-gold sequins across gentian
blue water, and glinting in your blue eyes.

A trolley ride, sunlight gleaming on the twin
tracks running before us in thin ribbons of

shining silver-gilt – we sway with the motion,
smile at each other – your hand rests on my knee . . .

and looking in your eyes as you move above
me, sunlight blazes in my unguarded heart.

For decades I am blind from once staring
into the sun's light reflected in your blue eyes.

Ashes

After the white fire, what is left? Finest powder
of pale gray ash – and the sly tears that come seeping when

I least expect, usually the times believing them
conquered at last. In those dark midnights, after eyes close

in sleep, a dream image recurs – a young woman from
a yesterday years past moving with such absurd, bright

expectation through her days after meeting Destiny's
appointed lover. But each time dreamed, while this figure

remains mirror-shine clear, her slender form appears
slightly smaller as I move farther from her down the

long gray tunnel of days increasing to decades since
one hour's golden encounter ignited the sparks

that flared to consuming white fire – and left a heart
enduringly scarred, and my days powdered with ash still

falling from charred hopes of the life a naïve fool
once imagined possible. Even now, you are

familiar as my own skin, near as the steady beat
of heart beneath – my dream of home in a summer

country forever out of reach that glimmers, star-lit,
distant beyond hope, through the blackest nights of the life
               I have been given.

Only one question for me at the end – so many years,
so many tears – were those moments beside you worth it?
               I would do it all again.

Another Country

The sight line to True Love is straight as arrow's flight,
striking deep to inmost soul and beating heart through
flesh, blood and tendon. When white Aphrodite smiles,

radiant sun breaks forth, lumining for two lovers
blossom-edged pathway to vine-trellised cottage in
summer garden where arrive golden mornings, slow,

shade-laced afternoons folding into velvet nights
sheened with shot-silk gleams of joy, desire, laughter,
and swift, rainbow-winged dreams, rose-scented, after.

   Love is another country.

But when a jealous god shapes happenstance to separate
lovers, straight line back to Heart's Desire there is
none . . . only obscure paths through dusky woods, thorny

bushes, mucky ditches and bramble patches, down
narrow-cleft chasms, up knife-blade cliffs and slipping
scree to craggy alpine passes while raw, cold green

springs of despair – gray days rain-streaked in rivers of
tears, weeks of black storm-clouded grief – plunge victim
direct into winter dark months of bone-shattering frost

  encasing spirit in a glazed, crazed ice coffin.

A child, brought north from golden days of sea and sun,
constructs thick carapace as protection in this new,
alien land of chill gray rain and cold white snow.

Growing, she finds refuge creating imagined
kingdoms where butterflies, wings shimmering jewel
colors in bright air, dance above rainbow-hued

flowers in sun-kissed gardens. Once a man arrives
from the distant, sun-burnt south, igniting for
a short span sun-struck love in a heretofore

undiscovered Paradise Garden, but soon he
leaves, and garden locked against her. Try as woman
may to return to gold-dusted sun country,

circumstance ever intervenes, defeating her.
But love of a younger man – weak in aspects yet
kind, gradually maturing, and wise in knowing

space must be made always for her drawings and tales –
provides a warming glow in her life utterly
different from previous, consuming gold-flecked flames,

thawing soul-oppressing ice layers some degree.
Over time, the scenes of sharp-cut peaks, fir trees
and the constantly shape-changing cloudscapes of

northern skies become beautiful in her eyes, and
some of her art inspired by the mountains,
hills, islands, trees, water always in view. One cool

late spring day she climbs trail up lower peak of
Olympic Range – seated on convenient rock she takes
in vista spread wide around her: fir-covered

indigo foothills below and to north and south,
while behind to west and on up north loom shade-blue
cliffs, crevasses and glare white snowfields of higher

summits cutting into rinsed blue where a few wisps
of cotton cloud drift and the brown wings of two
white-tailed, white-headed eagles scribe circles above

the peninsula's countless salt water inlets,
these shining silken surfaces reflecting tints
from transparent azure to dark cobalt. In this

blue and white day's light, on her Olympic peak,
the woman is convinced all has turned out for best and
she now dwells, full-content at last, as habitant of
    this country of the far north.

Recurring night dreams, however, tell another tale.
Again and again, in black midnights, I am returned
to blue and gold summer country, my steps skimming

spring soft grass sprinkled with tiny flowers of white
chamomile, pink thyme, blue speedwell, my limbs moving
through a golden radiance falling from an atmosphere

filled with scents of clove pinks, jasmine and rosemary,
a wren's piercing notes echoing from wild rose tangle.
There, if spirit-self has chosen right path that night,

one comes toward me through the gold-flecked air, figure
edged in luminous brilliance of gilt-white – the man
who belongs to this green-gold garden, this secret

    inmost part of me, this other country
  that lies still at the beating heart of my life.

Foreshadowings

The Tapestries in the Tower

I.

Pushing through heavy folds of dusty tapestry, a woman enters
topmost room in a stone tower. Dim, long light ribbons filter here and
there through fabric panels hanging from rings on a brass rod encircling

the entire space. Those lighter strips must indicate windows, the
woman thinks – crossing floor she thrusts one of these panels aside. Yes!
A high pointed window filled in small, clear panes, two narrower ones each

side disclosed, grand panoramas unrolling beyond. Moving swiftly
around the room, the woman slides the weighty woven stuff away from
all the casements, scrunching these panels into the tapestries hanging

in front of walls with a jangling of brass rings, pushing windows wide as
she progresses. Soon as she opens first glazed panes, transparent zephyrs
flow in from azure air outside, their silk-cool breaths slipping round
  woman's

arms, shoulders, neck, brushing her cheeks . . . eddying about room, the
  aery
sprites reach long fingers into every crevice, whisk out on a whim then
in, out again, their wayward gyrations fluttering her gown, teasing

gilt hair to fly about her face. When all windows stand open and space
flooded with light, she realizes the four glass-paned trios placed on main
compass points: starting with west triad, she gazes out for some minutes,

entranced, before continuing to north windows, then the east and
finally the south, drinking in the vast prospects stretching far as her
eyes can see – even, in two directions, unto indigo oceans.

Lower, under her sandaled feet, winking colors catch her glance – looking
down she finds the floor set with tesserae forming a large circle where
scenes of valleys, hills, mountains, forests, deserts, rivers, seas, islands,

harbors, towns and cities depicted in enamel tile chips – leaning
to study these, she finds the land and waterscapes strangely mimic those
she viewed from tower windows. Around this circle runs a wide band of

cobalt tiles – herein diamond, ruby, emerald, sapphire, topaz
gems glitter the outlines of zodiac constellations while centered
direct above the earth mosaic, at roof's steep apex, an immense

platinum chandelier of seven increasing tiers depends from
giant silver hook. As the woman stands, marveling, a strong south- east
gust suddenly spins into tower, whips once around the space then as

abruptly departs, all the leaded panes in succession crashing shut.
A laggard zephyr, trapped, puffs irritation, shoving tapestries back
over windows, rings clanging – the room swiftly shadows, grows black
  dark. . . .

II.

Direct above a thunderclap explodes – one narrow window cracks a bare
inch and zephyr escapes. As pane slams shut once more, second thunderclap
resounds and every wick on every candle of the great chandelier

ignites. Taking hands from ears, the woman looks around: the tapestries
shimmer slightly, the woven fabric brighter in candlelight, the draft
seeping between window panes and stone walls stirring figures now seen
  plain

to active life. Drawn to west tapestry, she examines it close: top and
bottom it displays motif of scarlet, perfect-shape hearts beside damaged
ones – some exhibit cracks, some jag-edged ones split in half, still

others rimmed black around gray centers – interspersed, a few white ones,
  rims
stitched in glinting gold or silver thread, centers sewn with sparkling crystals.
Curious about pattern, the woman counts: two perfect hearts then six

damaged ones, and last before repeat a single glittering white heart.
Turning, she scans others in the series of panels covering
windows and walls and sees all bordered with similar pattern of hearts

top and bottom . . . looking back to the one in front of her, she takes in
detailed landscapes and figures loomed between heart margins, discerning
   first
a girl-child with aureole of platinum-bright hair in sunlit rainbow

garden, tall white-haired woman beside; next she descries child wandering
alone, distressed, in dank forest beneath dripping rain-gray, cloud- layered
skies; in scenes following, child found in an alpine meadow, drawing

wildflowers on piece of white bark with burnt charcoal stick, chalet in
   distance;
next the woman beholds her in convent scriptorium, painting
with sable brush on vellum; after this, north window hanging reveals

slim figure a young maiden, gold hair braided in coronet, picking
flowers in bluebell wood, and a knight – tall, lean, hair sun-bleached brown,
   wearing
helm and blazoned surcoat over ring mail – is loomed into weave

astride a chestnut steed. Man and maid meet in the leaf-green, sun- dappled
wood and tapestry shows the twain walking together, conversing,
sharing bread, cheese, flask of wine man brings from saddlebags . . .
   subsequent,

these two enact love's ancient alchemy, melding for brief while into
one . . . soon after, the knight rides away, the maiden watching from hill as
man and horse disappear in dusk-blue twilight, the sky west orange streaked.

III.

In large panel following, the woman discovers the maid journeying,
in donkey cart toward a city – there she appears bent over table
in workshop, illuminating a manuscript; next, with leather scrip,

carrying staff, she is glimpsed among pilgrims taking ship over blue
sea, then walking, sometimes riding, with folk on roads across plain, forest,
moor and mountain, up dale and cliff, down ditch and crevasse, through
   valleys, bogs

and hedges, at times floating on rafts and boats over lakes, inlets and
rivers, paying her way by staying short whiles in different castles, towns,
cities, and using her precious array of fine brushes to paint

brilliant miniatures using colors and parchment given by clients
eager to purchase one of her enchanted vistas. As well these years,
sundry men seen companioning her at intervals, but none remain

long in scenes until older, plump merchant introduced. First shown as her
patron, he is next seen wedding her, then escorts her to fine town house
and up into tower which his pointing hand indicates her privy

workroom – from her own experience, woman regarding tapestry
infers this woman grown wearied of short-lived physical transactions,
desiring nothing more than to concentrate on her pictures. Glancing back

at the circling tapestries, the woman looking at tale displayed here
realizes in every one, after the maiden's encounter with the
knight, no matter her congress with other men or how many years passed,

the tapestries show her sometimes lifting head from work, a vision of
the knight's smile and summer blue eyes before her, or his remembered
form seen startling her awake in bed to find salt tears on her cheeks.

The woman looking sighs, steps to the next cloth square of the progression
which exhibits a great court funeral for beloved queen of the
country where the illuminator lives with her generous husband.

At this event, foredoomed, she meets her lost knight again – his brown hair
   now
silver-streaked and face more lined, but eyes the same piercing blue – and
   still
the smile that turns her breathless and makes her heart tremble in her
   breast.

The woman inspecting the textiles now approaches, trepidation
marked, the final, south panels . . . these disclose man and gilt-haired
  woman
together but their figures depicted in a foreign land, in a place

where they freely talk, clash, clasp for brief spell . . . then a tableau of
  woman's
husband welcoming her when she comes back. This pattern of leaving and
returning enacted several times – here the woman viewing these

episodes interprets: the knight, married, can never leave a dear and
ailing wife, and high in his sovereign's favor he is relied on
to lead battalions in spring campaigns – nor does woman in tapestry

wish to wound to heart's core her kind patron by permanent desertion.
Then two more tableaux: the lovers parting, and the woman with husband
again – and here the loomed cloth stops, snipped thread ends dangling long,
  untidy

fringe. Eyes tear-brimmed, heart hammering, the woman in the tower turns
  from
this Fate-wove tale of divided heart, divided lovers that reveals
no simple resolution – breath stifled, she hastes to nearest casement.

IV.

Lifting arms, she slides back rings from south windows, presses middle pane
  out –
instantly, a whirlwind blasts in, spinning on cyclone point around room –
the tapestries billow and flap, flying in woman's face, entangling

her limbs. Fighting her way through swirling folds, she finds oak door,
  pushes hard,
slips through, then – cautious in faint light – moves to step drop-off and
  starts down
a steep, spiral-twisting stone stair. On she continues, landing after

landing, thin slits in stone walls providing opaque light glimmers, moving
always lower and lower until she is walking down sloped incline
of polished tile then, standing on rubber escalator steps, is

carried farther down still. Reaching bottom at last, she crosses a
linoleum floor, wends way through crowds straight to tall, silver-haired man
waiting in appointed place – and is clasped safe in strong, longed-for arms.

For an achingly short, heart-break span, the woman is
again come home.

A Spirit, Wayfinding

There are no maps for journeys of the heart,
no cars, boats, trains or planes spirit may take to

its longed-for destination. Transport is
soul-ghost's silent steps dream-walking through star

strewn skies on nights a new moon sails heaven's
sapphire river in those hours before small

east wind spins silken air into pearl-white dawn . . .
other times voyaging occurs when drifting

mind-essence takes wing in the hour pale moths
flit, swirl and dance in the crystal dewfall of

>   quiet blue and lavender twilights.

Once discovery made of these enchanted,
uncharted lands of heart's desire, there is

never a way to call phantom-soul back,
only stubborn persistence trudging daytime's

weary track as earth-bound body blunders through
sticky webbings of dragging seconds, thick,

pricking forests of storm-shadowed, slow-ticking
hours, clotted swamps of weeks silting into

months-long morasses, and across steep slopes and
jagged ice fields of high-piled, glacier cold years.

During this wearing passage skin grows marred with
abrasions, cuts, scars until day body stopped by

fall through snow crust into crevasse or trip on
concealed log plunges it down to fanged rocks. If

anatomy endures to stand upright once
more, it wanders directionless, severed from

sense, in stony wilderlands for gray, uncounted aeons.

One woman-spirit, observing flesh and blood's
clumsy daylight progress from her skull-tethered

residence, waits impatient for release in
gauze twilights and black velvet nights when she

drifts free, wayfinding through every compass point
in quest of her heart's long-sought, ages-lost home.

As a certain violet-veiled eventide
melts into dark indigo, her ghost arrives

somewhere mist obscured as cloud-veiled star. Gliding
blind through rime-breathed fog's clutching fingers, death-chill

ice shard suddenly pierces her phantom spirit
and sky-ground dissolves from beneath her. She falls far

and farther, then hits head hard – a Bang! sounds
        loud in her ears – then nothing.

Waking by a dusty path, the woman
staggers to feet, reels forward under gray, hazed

sky and stumbles around a sharp bend. Here path
widens to a lane between columned poplars,

and as she walks the haze burns off and her route
becomes scattered with sun coins spilling through

twinkling green heart-shape leaves. Her bones straighten in
the warmth, and the mist clouding her mind fades . . .

walking faster, she spies in distance a stone
wall with scrolled iron gate between stout pillars,

moving toward it through flickers of shade
transparence and flakes of sifting gold dust.

At the gate she pauses, takes a breath before
lifting rusted latch. The stiff hinges refuse

to budge, but pushing with her whole strength hard
against one side, it yields – creaking protest – just

enough, and she slips inside. Feet skimming
grass, hands impatiently thrusting past branches

of overgrown shrubs and rampant vines twining
down from wood pergolas and great-limbed trees, she

searches, frantic, hurrying here and there till
arriving at way's meet of three close-mown paths

deep in the garden's fragrant, blossoming heart.

There, a weeping silver pear bends over a
fountain plashing diamond water drops,

and on topmost bough a speckle-breasted thrush,
head back, throat pulsing, pours from open beak

continuous staves of bright notes that suspend for
shining instants in the satin smooth air.

A tall, brown-haired man stands working near the tree,
digging over rich earth with long-haft shovel,

pots of pansy seedlings close by. At the
rustle of light steps he turns half-round,

crinkle-cornered eyes glancing intense blue, tanned
face brightening with never-forgotten smile.

   'What has kept you so long?' he asks.
She is come into her rightful dwelling place at last.

The Other Woman

Age stripping away delusion, I see the woman
more often now, in daylight and night dreams . . . about

my height, of similar figure and hair tint, clothed in
garments of antique years. I glimpse her to the side

of me, though always on branching track winding toward
distant hills – or just ahead, vanishing on curve screened

by dense thorn hedge – quick turning, sometimes I spot her not
far behind, disappearing into shadowed wood where

close-grown trunks conceal her from sight. Only at the end,
I've come to realize, will she hesitate, then

look at me full-face. Drawn close, side by side, our forms
will thin, waver into phantom transparence as

we commingle each into the other. Heart no
more severed from soul, nor the twain split by decades'

false trails, dead ends, muddy byways or pathless wastes,
this figure, clothed in golden radiance, begins

her long walk home, fearlessly stepping forth onto
the star roads that blaze white fire through blackest nights.

Pale Shades and Star Roads

Down the starry pathways hasten the Messenger's wingèd feet, each
hour bearing nearer the Fate decreed spear with flame-forged tip
that once thrown will slice cold iron between us, beginning the time
        when you forget and I remember.

I – Altar of the Gods

A columned temple stands atop sheer cliff rising from cyan blue
sea, its sculpted marble altar veined in silver and gold. Kneeling
before it, linen mantle covering sun-gilt hair, a woman

petitions for the dearest aspiration of her star-born soul,
and the hope of every heart's beat left her on the cloud-wrapped earth.
        Her silent prayer to the temple's god framed thus:
       'Wherever my beloved is, whoever with – I would be in

a blossoming tree's thin gray shades moving on pavement where he steps
one blue-rinsed spring morning – and pauses, memory snagged on other
place where like silhouettes once lightly caressed a slim form,
        slender, tapered fingers clasped in his . . .

the cloud shadows flowing over long grass, the sigh of summer wind
rustling oak leaves some warm afternoon and catching his thought with
brief vision of crossing a meadow holding a fine-boned hand on
        similar day in the lost long ago . . .

the gossamer brush of gauzy cloth as he bends over pink and white
butterfly flowers, breathing evanescent scent that sends his mind
questing ghostly image from almost forgotten scene hid behind
        curtaining mist of vanished years . . .

a whispered voice in echo-bare room of whitewashed hillside house in
white town by white sand shore – where soon as he enters, quick shifting
head to cast glance here, there, the haunting, half-familiar sibilance
        drifts away in resin-scented air . . .

soft footfall on cobbled street and glimpse of fluttering skirt that
suddenly recalls a woman long since disappeared, but fast as
he walks, beyond corner turn the figure gone without trace, eclipsed
in black passage or dark door arch . . .

a branch tap-tapping at casement window on a stormy night that
causes him to glance up from lamp-lit book, momenty envision
nebulous shade from distant, bygone age, then shake his head as vague
illusion evaporates to nothing. . . .'

II – Celestial Pathways, Starry Meadows

Mortality's bonds loosed, a spirit woman walks forward into black,
fathomless void hung with planet-spanning swathes of deep-pile velvet.
As she moves, the thick dark gradually thins, transforms to a gray zone

webbed in clinging veils of shiver-silk vapor . . . a phosphor-limned stair
dimly emerging, the faint-outlined shape begins ascending to
the hazed, star-seeded firmament. Slowly, wreathing fog disperses,

revealing a path among stars now blazing diamond fire where the
near-transparent wraith, hair a platinum aureole, treads over faceted,
refractive crystals and metallic iridescent scales, some edged

daisy rays centered with tiny spinning gold suns, some with myriads
of atmosphere-blue forget-me-not flakes, topaz star motes winking
in each minute flower. At times the slight shade steps from this glowing

celestial track to wander luminescent star fields stretching
to measureless infinities where, entranced, she gathers great
bouquets – coruscating lily-shape clusters of astral dust, opal

blooms of boreal effulgence, sparkling rainbow roses flung from
fissioning atom bursts, spiky sprays of spectrum-sparking dazzle
cast from streaking comets' unfurling wakes and the falling tinsel
glitter of continual meteor showers. . . .

III – The Garden beyond the Stars

However far this phantom woman ranges, shining memory
of a man's smile blazoned on her soul guides her always back to
ordained path and on through the million mazed crossing ways – day bright

and night murk, intriguing, seductive – constantly splintering
away on either side. She travels far and farther, hours and
aeons passing, till instant an infinitesimal ion

flashes – a miniscule crack fractures an escarpment of stony
eternity and seconds sheer off epochs' towering granite cliffs.
A clear, cut-glass bell tone sounds – the woman, startled, turns and as the

echo fades, down a star-daisy bordered path not noticed before,
she discerns portal where small white flower-petal spheres swarm and burn.
In front of this radiant arch, a man's tall, silver-haired figure

stands, glimmer-gold scintillae raining through ether around him – each
twinkling grain cast from waves in the cosmic tides flowing through
fathomless atmosphere deeps of endless empyrean's boundless

ocean arriving to crest and break here, in this moment, this place,
and powder the man, then the shock-stilled woman in swirling drifts
of shimmering golden molecules.

Eternal instants pass . . .
planets wheel and collide, suns implode and are born anew . . .
your eyes, surprised, interlock with mine –
your gaze sharpens, and my beloved begins walking toward me –
the woman with hair an aureole of palest gilt.

The Asphodel Meadow

At that star-flared instant at the very end –
or the moment after – you will walk toward me

across a steep slanting meadow filled with
six-petalled white asphodels set beneath

knife-blade limestone peaks, their sharp spires pricking
night sky thick sown with bright star fields where countless

millions of astral diamonds bloom, scattering
their light-refracting gilt-white pollen embers

through lost aeons' black-veiled depths to create
a star-powdered backdrop for your measured steps.

There is only the sound of a small wind
wandering among pinnacles star-transformed

to platinum ghosts, and the stiff rustle of
leaves and stems as you move to the place

I stand. Your hair is completely white, mine
gone silver-sand. I reach to touch your face –

you bend, briefly brush lips against mine, then
we lie together among the tall spikes of

star-pillared asphodel, and the strong green
scent of their broken stalks fills the air.

note: in Greek myth the Asphodel is associated with death and thought to grow in fields where spirits of those recently dead wander for a time.

Silver Rose & Handkerchief

Coda

Cavalier of the Rose
to Agnes Baltsa, Octavian, Salzburg, 1984

Act II

The white-haired maestro brings down his wand –
the red curtain opens, revealing:

High-ceilinged Baroque salon, young Sophie gowned in tight-laced, low-cut bodice
over gathered, layered petticoats and draped pink skirt, rose-festooned, that
bells and sways as she paces and turns in tremulous anticipation.

Eight footmen and major-domo enter, the Cavalier following
swiftly after – he stops centered between tall glass doors atop polished
parterre steps: a slim, upright figure, one hand on silver rapier's hilt,

the other holding aloft ritual silver rose. For extended moment
he poses – a fairytale prince costumed in white and silver from head to toe:
waved white queue-tied wig, diamond pin dazzling in foam of white cravat lace,

more wide lace at wrists, white damask waistcoat and long, deep-cuffed jacket
embroidered in lashings of silver thread winking with faceted crystals,
white satin knee breeches, white hose, heeled white shoes with sparkling crystal rosettes. . .

when the Cavalier paces forward the first shimmers of the silver
rose theme begin . . . he sings the presentation, half turns, offers the rose
to the girl – herself a new-opening rose in her petal pink gown,

smooth skin faintly flushed, neck encircled with pearls of palest pink innocence.
Receiving the gift, Sophie looks up to Octavian – their eyes meet . . .
lost in each other's gaze, the axis of their world shifts, time suspends . . .

Sophie sings the rose bearing its love-message must have been plucked from
a paradise garden, scent so strong it has caught her heart in a trap –
she is fearful as if standing on heaven's threshold, though even at risk

of dying she longs to stay in this strange place . . . she asks the Cavalier
if he has ever known such fragrance . . . captivated, he steps beside her,
bending his head to the rose – then looks up into her face, his dark eyes

intent, while delicate cascades of silver notes infuse every air mote
falling around the dazed pair, the music's vibrant harmonics transforming
the atmosphere into a coruscating effulgence of purest joy.

Tall angels in cloud spun blue-white gowns in-wove with silver lightning
  threads,
floss fine silver-white hair bright aureoles around heads, great plumed wings
  tinted
iridescent pearl and dove-gray shades, move about their celestial

garden, gently shaking dew-diamond roses to release a mist of
saffron-gilt pollen that drifts, sifts down to envelop the Fate-destined
lovers in a fragranced, gold-spangled haze only their star-filled eyes perceive.

Sophie, voice aspiring heavenward, sings that now he is near, fear is
changed to perfect bliss, wondering where she has felt such enchantment
  before . . .
Octavian's voice joins, echoing her astonishment at such unforeseen

happiness, singing her face and shining eyes brought this moment he will
  not
forget long as he lives, each asking if it does not seem this has happened
before in some beautiful dream, voices entwined while chiming strains of

harp, flutes, violins, celeste fountain over their rapture, Octavian
concluding his heart and soul will remain hers for all eternity.

Act III

Near act's end, plot complexities uncoil, irrelevancies falling
away – servants, commissioner, police, oafish suitor, girl's father –
at last the Cavalier kisses the Marschallin's outstretched hand – she exits.

Freed, Octavian turns at once to his love, arms opening wide to
enfold all the world in his Sophie – embracing him, the handkerchief
she has been clutching drops unheeded while showers of glittering notes

rain once more over the close-clasped lovers . . . Octavian sings only
if this happens to you can you believe it possible – unable
to contain welling exhilaration he moves center stage, expressing

amazed delight Fate contrived their meeting . . . Sophie marvels at his laughing
mood – she is fearful and weak as if come to heaven's threshold, needing
him to hold her. He returns to her side and their phrases interweave,

rising through an effervescing stream of scintillating, silver-sequined staves
that spill around them as they tell each other of feeling only
the beloved's touch and seeing only the dear one's face – everything else

is an unreal dream, their only reality being together and
knowing they will be joined for ever and ever. The last note achieved,
Octavian takes Sophie's hand, leading her to stair – on top step he kisses

her, then they walk together down the dark hall . . . the door at the far end
opens and they move through into a brief-seen, gilded luminescence.
    Immediately the door shuts behind them.

We are left in the dark, bereft. Of grace, the composer grants us brief
respite: the Marschallin's page runs onstage seeking the dropped handkerchief.
Watching, we begin adjusting to the cold mundane again, remind

ourselves the young couple's pitch-perfect, angel-conspired bliss hopeless
to sustain in this imperfect world . . . only in fairytale, ballet
or opera land can lovers walk hand in hand down a dim corridor

*into a pulsing aureate glow beyond a tight shut door. Though we
yearn to believe, blood and bone are weighted with certain foreknowing that
soon or late each of us must grope through that midnight passage alone to*

*discover if, on door's other side, an unfathomed alchemy transform
smother-velvet black to a limitless, airy zone suffused in a
soft yet lucent citron radiance glimmering over crystal streams*

*and flowered meadows scattered with arcing rainbow bridges and curving
paths into mist-glamoured distance where, on high crag of jagged, ice-bright,
snow-white peaks, amidst flowing gentian, lilac, smoke-gray clouds rimmed in*

*platinum-gilt nimbuses, a spired citadel is glimpsed,
heart's-gold fire arrows flashing from the gilded, peaked roofs of
its countless halls, turrets, belfries, and soaring towers.*

Colophon

This book was edited and designed by Jeffrey Copeland at Bywater Press, Bellingham, Washington during the fall and winter of 2018–2019. The text is Adobe Garamond, with Kuenstler Script as the display type. The book was set using the TeX typesetting system and custom-developed software for automatically converting files from Microsoft Word to TeX.

Garamond is an old-style typeface based on the designs of French typesetter and designer Claude Garamont (1480–1561) early in the age of moveable type. The Adobe version used here was designed by Robert Slimbach in 1989, at the beginning of the age of desktop publishing. Kuenstler Script is a 1989 Linotype interpretation of a 1902 Stempel design *Künstlerschreibschrift* – "handwriting of artists."

TeX was developed by mathematician and computer scientist Donald Knuth. It was originally released in 1978 and intended for printing mathematical textbooks, however, it is equally suited for high-quality, general-purpose typesetting.

The high-resolution scans of Ms Bayley's art used within this volume and on its cover were made by Carl Cooper at Color 1 Photo of Seattle.

www.bywaterpress.com